❧ Lessons from Ground Zero

2003

For Isaac

Love

Walt.

広島

Lessons from Ground Zero

❧ *A Hiroshima and Nagasaki Story*

WALTER ENLOE

Illustrations by Serene Enloe and Isaac Enloe
Contributions from Nicholas Kashman
and St. Paul Avalon High School students

HAMLINE UNIVERSITY PRESS
Saint Paul, Minnesota
2002

Hamline University
St. Paul, Minnesota 55104

Printed in the United States of America

ISBN 0-9633686-9-9

Library of Congress Control Number 2002108122

To the children and future leaders and to the teachers and students of Hiroshima International School, especially Mayumi Yingling, Sakae Nakai, Kim Blackford, Yuri Kim, and Nicole Thompson.

In honor of my peacemaking teachers, Kawamoto-san, Nobori-san, Shibama-san, Tanimoto-san, Yaguchi-san, and Nagai-san.

With thanks to friend and editor Stacey Lynn and to old friend and noted author Pat Conroy, who helped me find my voice as a teacher and a writer.

To my friend Ken Simon, who led me to the Oasis of Peace, and to Emily Miller and Raina Fox, who gave me insights and support.

A special thanks to Dan Loritz and Hamline University for their support of teacher-storytellers.

Thanks to the Peace Resource Center, Wilmington College, for their work and for permission to quote from their translations of In the Sky over Nagasaki *and* Living Beneath the Atomic Cloud.

And most important, to my family: Kitty, Isaac, and Serene, and my parents, Winton and Kitty Enloe, who brought me to Japan.

Contents

1. The School on the Mountain *1*
2. The First Interviews *21*
3. Nuclear Nightmares *36*
4. Peace Park Ceremony *51*
5. A New Beginning *64*
6. The Study Begins *83*
7. Dean and Isaac's Story *107*
8. Radiation *118*
9. Peace Walk through the City of Death *131*
10. Life and Death Questions *154*
11. Searching for Truth *162*
12. Life Ain't Fair *178*
13. Truth Is Stranger Than Fiction *195*
14. Birds of Peace *222*
15. The 1000 Cranes Club *231*

Resources *236*

❧ International Decade for a Culture of Peace and Nonviolence

On November 10, 1998, the United Nations General Assembly, accepting the appeal of every living Nobel Peace Prize laureate, proclaimed 2001–2010 to be the International Decade for Constructing a Culture of Peace and Nonviolence for the Children of the World. A culture of nonviolence values love, compassion, and justice. It rejects violence as a means of solving problems and embraces communication, cooperative decision making, and nonviolent conflict resolution. It insures freedom, security, and equitable relationships. It promotes inner peace, personal transformation, and disarmament.

This book celebrates the longest-standing sister-city relationship between Japan and the United States: Nagasaki, Japan, and St. Paul, Minnesota. It also honors the new sister-university relationship between Hamline University in St. Paul (Minnesota's oldest university, celebrating 150 years in 2004) and Kwassui University in Nagasaki (Japan's oldest university for women). Both universities are affiliated with the United Methodist Church.

❧ I

The School on the Mountain

It was a hot, humid morning in late July 1985. At the main train station in Hiroshima, several students waited for the 8:20 A.M. bus that would take them through the suburbs to the International School. Built on the side of a mountain, the school overlooks the Ota River, which flows toward the city into six streams that empty into Japan's Seto Inland Sea. Hiroshima, meaning "wide islands," is largely built on the human-made islands, or enlarged deltas, that sit in the estuaries where fresh water meets the salty sea.

In a week, the school would recess for a month. This morning, as on most mornings, students rode trains from throughout the area to the main station. There they would catch a bus to school. Niraj lived close to Hiroshima National University Hospital, where his father, a surgeon from India, was studying micro hand surgery. Niraj walked fifteen minutes to the neighborhood station to board a train for downtown. Americans Mia and Mai lived in the countryside and took a taxi to their local train station. Heather lived near the main station and walked to the bus stop each morning, just as she did in her hometown of Melbourne when she was there. Harold, originally from Holland, lived on an island in the Inland Sea. He took a hydrofoil to the Ujina Port and then a bus to the main station. Most of the hundred or so children attending the International School lived far from each other, within a radius of about thirty-five miles of the school.

The bus driven by Yaguchi-san arrived precisely at 8:20 and the merry, motley crew took off through the mountain valley. The road followed the meandering river to the school, referred to by students as "The Island."

The school is open year round except for several weeks in late August, and students usually study three out of the four terms. Most teachers and students return to their home countries during one of the terms for a winter or summer vacation. Each year, the small, close-knit group, grades K–9, is composed of students from some fifteen countries, the population varying depending on the business climate in Japan. Many of the parents work with Mazda and Ford Motor companies or with Mitsubishi Heavy Industries. Others are teachers, professors, or missionaries, and there is the occasional professional baseball player for the Hiroshima Carp. Some parents are researchers or physicians with the Radiation Effects Research Foundation (originally the Atomic Bomb Casualty Commission), which studies the effects of nuclear radiation on the victims of the atomic bombings in Hiroshima and Nagasaki on August 6 and August 9, 1945.

The school also serves hundreds of part-time students. Most are Japanese, but some are foreigners studying English and Japanese language and culture. In addition, about fifty "returnees," Japanese students who have lived at least three years in an English-speaking country and attended a Japanese school, come to the International School on Thursday and Saturday afternoons.

❧ Boxes of Birds

Over the past several years, the post office had delivered to the school many boxes addressed to Peace Park, Hiroshima, Japan, or Children's Monument, Hiroshima. Just in the last month, parcels had arrived from Portland, Oregon; Vancouver, Canada; and Hopkins, Minnesota. Inside each box were hundreds of brightly colored paper birds. Students at the International School would string the birds into garlands to be hung at the monuments in Peace Park. No one was exactly sure how this yearly project of stringing cranes from distant lands had started, but it had become a tradition. Students and teachers had read Eleanor Coerr's book *Sadako and the 1000 Paper Cranes* or other versions of Sadako's story, and they liked the idea of folding a thousand cranes for peace.

As every student at the school knew, Sadako Sasaki was only two years old when the atomic bombing destroyed Hiroshima and her home. At age twelve, Sadako became ill with the "A-bomb disease," or leukemia. With the help of her friends, she folded a thousand paper cranes, which, according to Japanese folklore, would guarantee a long life. Following Sadako's death in 1955, her classmates created the Paper Crane Club and initiated a worldwide movement to raise funds to build the Children's Monument in Peace Park. The monument was completed in 1958.

Now the senior level (grades 6–8) students at the International School sat on the floor of the media center on this

sultry summer day. Using light fishing line and small darning needles, they strung crane after crane, creating rainbow strands of fifty colored-paper symbols of hope and peace. After stringing the cranes, students made banners in English and Japanese proclaiming the contributing schools' names and locations. Then the principal and interested students took a bus downtown to Peace Park to hang the cranes at the Children's Monument in the center of the park.

❧ Commentators on Hiroshima

Later that afternoon Dean and Yoshio's dad, Mr. Leeper, and Aisha's father, Mr. Wiig, came to the school. They were both university teachers in Hiroshima and translators of Japanese into English. Like many of the parents in the school, Steve Leeper and Lonnie Wiig liked living in Japan. That was one reason all students studied Japanese language and culture, including origami, or paper-folding.

Steve said to the students, "Lonny Wiig and I came to school today to ask you to help us with two peacemaking projects. You know that Thursday is August 6, the day of the peace ceremony at Peace Park. In the evening, people float the lanterns down the Ota River. This year's commemoration is much bigger and more significant than past ceremonies. It's the fortieth anniversary of the bombing of Hiroshima, and the worldwide press coverage will be unprecedented."

"Why is that, Leeper-san?" asked Nicole, a recent arrival from Australia. Nicole used the Japanese word *san,* which was like saying "mister."

"One reason is that the world is full of nuclear weapons.

The United States and the Soviet Union are still deeply involved in a cold war," Steve said.

"MAD is what it is," Mr. Wiig added. "M.A.D. is an acronym. The initials stand for Mutual Assured Destruction. Both countries are poised to blow up each other and the rest of the world."

"Sounds like a hot war, not a cold war," Isaac said. Isaac was from the United States and had lived in Japan more than six years. His dad, Walter Enloe, was principal of the International School, and his mom taught there.

Mrs. Mayumi Yingling, the Japanese culture teacher, added, "Hiroshima is also a symbol of peace. It is the International City of Peace and Culture, and people come here to make plans for global peacemaking. Every year is an important commemoration. The fortieth has no particular significance for Japanese people, but for Westerners it does. Perhaps for Americans it is similar to celebrating birthdays—something that we Japanese do not do."

Mai, who was now fourteen and had been at the international school eight years, asked the big question. "Specifically, what do you want us to do?"

"Well, Mai," Steve said, "you've got several choices. Lonny will share one in a minute. I'm inviting you to volunteer to be interviewed by reporters and journalists for radio, TV, and newspapers from throughout the world."

"What exactly do we do?" Isaac asked.

"Do you two remember several years ago when the whole school went to Peace Park to meet Pope John Paul II?" Steve asked.

"Yes," said Isaac. "I was really impressed that he could speak in at least nine languages."

"That was cool," Steve continued. "Remember after the speech you went to meet Cardinal Carsoli, the Secretary of State of the Vatican?"

"He asked us about living in Hiroshima," Isaac said.

"And he also wanted to know how we students were peacemakers," Mai added.

"Right," Steve went on. "Remember how you were interviewed by the press?"

"I remember all the lights and microphones and cameras and stuff," Mai said.

"What did you talk about?" Kino asked.

"I don't really remember. It was just so embarrassing," Mai replied.

"Movie star!" Isaac teased.

"Jealous?" retorted Mai's best friend, Mia.

"Okay, be calm," Steve interjected. "What I remember most vividly is Mai quoting from the Pope's speech: 'To remember the past...'"

"To remember the past is to commit oneself to the future. To remember Hiroshima is to abhor nuclear war. To remember Hiroshima is to commit oneself to peace." She closed her eyes. She remembered. The room was quiet.

"Cool," Mia whispered.

"Very cool," agreed Isaac.

"Well done, Mai. This time the press wants to interview American kids living in Hiroshima in conjunction with the fortieth anniversary," Steve said.

"How about Nagasaki?" Emma asked.

"Few foreigners live there," replied Mr. Rehlin. "There is no international school. A part-time student from Holland who lives in Nagasaki will begin studying here next month."

"Who?" asked Emma.

"A girl named Andrea."

Now the room was buzzing with chatter.

Curtis yelled out, "How about us Aussies and Kiwis, mate?"

Johann matched him in volume, "I am the sole Swedish representative of my government in western Japan. I must have a voice."

"Mr. Ambassador," Isaac said.

Mai joined the chorus of voices, "Will they want to interview us next year?"

"Probably not," Kino said. "This is our big chance."

"But you're not American, Kino," Johann said.

"I'm double and international," he replied. Kino was half Japanese and half New Zealander—this is what he meant by "double." Most of the students who had lived in Japan more than a year called themselves international.

Mr. Leeper spoke up. "Listen up. Everybody gets to participate. We'll find ways for everyone to be interviewed. There are press people from every place in the world except Antarctica. The first calls have been for American kids."

All the students were used to being different. They stood out in a country where everyone else was Japanese. They were used to being stared at, talked about, the center of attention. They were often called "gaijin" by the Japanese, a word that literally means "outsider" and is used negatively, in the way that some people might say "Jap" or "Nip."

"Attention everybody," Mr. Rehlin intoned through hands cupped like a megaphone. "All Australians, British, Canadians, Indians, New Zealanders, and English-speaking wannabees. This afternoon we will begin lessons in American

English pronunciation, specifically the accent from my hometown, Dallas, Texas."

The room filled with boos and yelps and laughter.

Curtis tried to imitate Mr. Rehlin, "Yeh suuuuhhhh, Mista Raylynn."

Mr. Leeper jumped in. "Mr. Rehlin is right. We will find ways for everyone to participate. Now let's hear from Mr. Wiig."

"Some of you know that for the last five years we've helped to organize the Hiroshima Peace Day broadcast," began Lonny Wiig. "Each August 6 we broadcast the peace ceremony and the mayor's peace message throughout the world. We are on all the radio stations for children as well as rock stations. Last year we were on public radio in fifty-six countries. This year we're expanding the program to other countries and adding a student component. I'm inviting you to try out to be announcers and commentators for our new International Kids' Network Program next Thursday. We'll need four people. All students are welcome."

"Wow," Kino said. "Can I do it in Japanese?"

Lonny replied, "You can try out, Kino, but the Kids' Network will only be in English this year. It's sponsored by a group in Australia, where the tape will go. The program will be broadcast worldwide from there."

"Henna," said Kino, using a slang word that meant *weird*, "but okay."

Mrs. Yingling added, "By tomorrow we should have other invitations, because this next week will also be the celebration of the United Nations' International Year of Youth, and there will be hundreds of representatives to the First World Conference of Mayors for Peace. So be prepared."

Steve said, "Okay, let's break into groups. People who want to be interviewed by the press, meet in the commons in five minutes. People who want to try out for broadcasting, meet Lonny upstairs in the music room. It's soundproof, so it should be like a broadcasting booth. Everyone bring a notebook and a pencil. Let's go."

Mariko and Janelle sat at a corner table working with the cranes. "My English is not good enough, I don't think," said Mariko, a Japanese returnee from Great Britain.

"I think it is. Your English is a hundred times better than my Japanese," Janelle replied. She had lived in Hiroshima nine months.

"John, we want to stay here and finish the cranes."

"Great," Mr. Rehlin said. "I'll stay too. Mrs. Yingling will help us letter the banners in Japanese."

❧ Practicing

"Talk right through it. Don't look at the microphone. See beyond it," Mr. Wiig emphasized as the students sat at a table with an array of microphones. "Speak in your normal voice at a normal level. We'll let the microphones do their work so you don't have to speak loudly."

"What should we talk about?" Mai asked.

"We'll decide that in just a second. First let's do a sound check. Each person should talk into the microphone and speak clearly." Mr. Wiig showed them where to turn the microphones on.

"Haro, haro, bakaaro," Kino screeched, making fun of the way Americans sometimes imitate the Japanese. His rendition of "Hello, hello, stupid" made everyone laugh, including Mr. Wiig.

"Thanks, Kino, but no thanks. Here's what I want the six of you to do. I'll write it up here on the board. I want you to say your name, where you're from, how old are you, how long you've lived in Japan, and either what your parents do here or one thing you like about Hiroshima," Mr. Wiig said.

"Can we write it down?" Junior asked.

"Good idea," Mr. Wiig said, "because you need to think through what you might say. Also, most of what we do on the radio program will be prepared ahead of time and we will read it."

The students spent a few minutes writing, then Mr. Wiig said, "Okay, who's first? Go ahead, Mai."

"I'm Mai Russell. I'm fourteen years old and I'm from Seattle, Washington. I'm Japanese American. I've lived in Hiroshima eight years, and my dad is the chief radiologist at RERF."

"Excellent. Strong voice. Articulate," Lonny Wiig said.

"Booooo-teee-ful!!" said Kino.

"Kino, you're next then," Mr. Wiig said.

"Well, hi," Kino said in his deepest voice. He caught Mr. Wiig's eye and quickly returned to almost normal. "I'm Kino Millar. I'm half New Zealander and half Japanese. I've lived here all my life except for a year each in England and New Zealand. My parents are teachers, and I love the mountains and rivers by my house."

"Very strong, Kino. It's amazing what you're capable of," Lonny commented, winking at Kino. "Booooo-teee-ful, too. And only thirteen years old."

Next came Christina.

"I'm Christina Jossang. I'm fourteen years old. I'm from Oslo, Norway. I live here for two years now. My father is an engineer and my mother stays home or helps here at the school. I love the islands of Hiroshima."

"Nice job, Chris. Your intonation is perfect," Mr. Wiig commented.

"I'll go next," Curtis said. "Good day, mates. I'm Curtis Longman from Geelong, Australia. Me dad works for Ford. He's a designer. Latest job was the hubcaps on the new Probe. We've lived here eighteen months and I like you blokes most of all. Can't wait to go home next week for a vacation, although it'll be in the middle of winter."

"Poor child," Mai said. "May we offer you mittens?"

"Thanks, Curtis. Junior, you're next."

"Yes, I'm Junior from Salvador in Brazil. I'm fourteen and I live here almost a year. Muito bem!! My father is a Mitsubishi engineer, and my mother is staying in the home waiting for me. I like Japanese girls too. And you, and you, too," he said, blowing kisses and pointing at Mai and Christina and Mrs. Yingling as she walked into the room with Steve Leeper.

"You're so kind, Junior," Mrs. Yingling said, blowing him a kiss.

"Oh brother," whispered Mai to Christina, who nodded in agreement.

"Good morning, all. I'm Nicola Ashton from Durban, South Africa. My mum's from London, England. I'm thirteen and have lived here for three years, as my dad works with Mazda and Ford Motor. I like to study traditional karate and Japanese."

"Very good," Lonny exclaimed.

❧ Instructions

Now Steve Leeper spoke up. "Here I have copies of the English translation for this year's mayor's address. It's long, but I had fun translating it with my colleague Michiko. I think the best thing we can do is to divide it up and practice reading it. But first let me set the stage.

"We will be in the broadcast booth that sits about fifty meters from the area of the ceremony, which takes place in that large area between the museum and the cenotaph.[1] We're off to the right. The booth will have seats for four people and there will be four microphones. We begin at 8:10 and we will describe the scene—the weather, the people, the mood of the crowd. At 8:15 a bell will ring and then the mayor will give his Peace Declaration address, which will last for maybe ten minutes. Then choirs will sing and priests will pray. While the mayor is speaking we will read his address in English. Afterward I'll ask you a few questions. We will finish at 8:35."

"This doesn't look difficult," Christina said, reading from the script. "August 6, 1985. No more Hiroshimas. It was forty years ago today during the hot summer that the heat waves, fiery blast, and radiation emitted by the first nuclear weapon..."

"Slow down, Christina. Good voice level and pronunciation. Just speak at regular your pace," Mr. Leeper suggested.

---

1. The cenotaph is a repository for the names of those who have died over the years from the effects of the atomic bomb.

"...and radiation emitted by the first nuclear weapon ever used against a human target burned all living things in a blinding flash and turned the city of Hiroshima into a plain of scorched rubble."

Curtis commented, "This is very heavy stuff."

"It's somber," said Mrs. Yingling, "and yet full of hope as you read on. It is a plea to the world that there be no more Hiroshimas ever again."

"And no more Sadakos who have to suffer," Christina said. "And all the others too," she added.

"For the next fifteen minutes I want you to read through the Peace Declaration, first silently, then out loud," said Mr. Leeper. "After that we'll need to think about our commentary on the Peace Ceremony—before, during, and afterward. Go to it." Steve then turned to Mrs. Yingling and asked, "How is the other group doing?"

"Fine," she said. "They started off thinking of the wackiest questions the reporters might ask and then gradually they got more serious."

❧ Choosing the Questions

Down in the commons area, John Rehlin and Walter Enloe were writing feverishly, trying to get down all the questions students came up with in the second brainstorming session. Next they would classify and sort. The idea was to think of the kinds of questions reporters might ask and then prepare some thoughtful responses. Before every field trip or excursion, including home stays with sister Japanese schools, the senior- and middle-level students prepared for the trip, often with brainstorming sessions.

Across the top of the white board in large red letters was written

QUALIFY QUALIFY QUALIFY MOST IS BETTER THAN EVERYBODY SOME IS BETTER THAN ALL.

The questions students had listed, covering a wide range of possibilities, followed the senior level's rules for brainstorming: all ideas are allowed; no put-downs; piggy-backing is okay, but no elaboration/comments on other people's ideas until after the brainstorming session. And the most important guiding factor in this case, as articulated by Johann, "Let's put up only intelligent, reasonable questions asked by reasonable adult reporters to us reasonable students."

Niraj was saying something in Hindi. "Wow!" he said.

"What did you say?" Johann asked.

"You have the world by the tail, you great Swede," Niraji replied.

"Thank you, humble master," Johann said, bowing with hands clasped in respect.

Harold interjected, "Hey guys, let's organize these questions, or we may look bad with these reporters. The last time I was with my Dad's team, the reporters were as foolish as the players." Harold's father, Hans Ooft, a former star of European football (called soccer in the United States), was coach of the highly acclaimed Mazda football club, which played in the Japan League.

Dean added, "I was interviewed twice last year for the Peace Festival and once about bullying in the Japanese school I went to before coming here. It was really cool. The reporters were knowledgeable and very sympathetic."

"For your Japanese talk?" Isaac asked.

"No, they really seemed to understand what it must be like to be a gaijin."

The class erupted into yowls and catcalls. The word *gaijin* always set off a group of foreigners in Japan. In a minute the group settled down.

Though the students thought that empathy might well be impossible, especially for reporters from other countries asking about living in Japan, they agreed to do the best they could to communicate their perspectives.

Johann continued, "You know, at least in my country, adults can ask to kids some very stupid questions." The group feeling was that this was in fact universal, at least on this planet.

"Okay, who's going to sort these questions?" Steve asked. Isaac raised his hand to say that he would.

The group had listed some twenty-five questions. Isaac went to the board to set up the sorting and categorizing system the class used for social studies inquiry. On the board were five colored cards. The questions were written on white cards with a sticky back so they would stick to the whiteboard. The idea was to sort the questions into five groups (if possible) and then later to label each group. The students went at it with great skill, which came from months of practice. Isaac quickly put the five category cards, with their questions, on the board.

The students also created a sixth group that was a catch-all for anything that didn't seem to fit anywhere else but wasn't discarded. Questions such as "What is the secret of life?" and "Do you eat raw fish?" went into this category.

"Okay, I need everybody's help," John said. "Pair up with a friend, and I'll come around and assign you a

Living in Hiroshima	Japanese People	Going to School in Hiroshima	The A-bomb	Personal/ School
What do you like/ not like about Japan?	How do Japanese people treat you?	What is it like going to an inter-national school?		Where are you from?
How do you spend your free time?	Do you have Japanese friends?	What do you study? Do you study peace?		How old are you?
What's it like to live in the A-bomb city?	Have you met hibakusha?[2]	Do you study World War II?		What do your parents do?
How is Hiroshima the Inter-national City of Peace?		What do you think about the U.S. drop-ping the bomb on Hiroshima and Naga-saki?		How long have you lived here?

2. Hibakusha are bomb victims.

question. Remember our ground rules. Use 'I' statements, qualify your remarks, and be clear and direct. Avoid 'ahs' and 'ums' in your delivery, and by all means, avoid responses that lack reasoned thought. In other words, just be the geniuses I know you to be."

Mr. Enloe continued, "Tomorrow morning, first thing, we will have a meeting to review these questions and pool our resources. We'll type these up and use them as our info sheets. Also think about what questions or responses might be missing."

❧ Something Is Missing

The students went to work. Several minutes later Isaac noted in his Atlanta drawl, "Excuse me, but do y'all notice something weird on the board? Somethin's missing."

"You know, there's nothing in the A-bomb category," Johann exclaimed.

"Should we move some of the questions over to that group?" Harold asked.

"It's both strange and interesting that we didn't put anything in that category," Niraji commented.

"Well, we better think of something," Mia said. "That's the reason we're doing all this stuff, isn't it?"

"Really? I thought we were telling them about the good life in Hiroshima!" Dean chimed in.

"Seriously," Mia continued, "they probably want to know what foreign kids living in the A-bomb city think about the A-bomb."

Isaac added, "The great American question."

"I think it's more than that," Dean interjected.

"It's a 'down under' question too. In Australia we have Hiroshima Peace Day," said Heather.

"It's the world's problem," Yuri quietly added.

"What do we know?" Dean asked. "I don't know much about the bomb. It doesn't exactly come up in conversations with my friends."

"I've been to the Peace Museum once," Janelle said. "It's all about war and suffering. It made me sick."

"I've lived here for a long time now," Niraj said, "and I'm not going in there yet."

"In Holland we do not study such subject except war history in the high school," Harold said.

Johann added, "In Sweden they do at age fourteen, because my brother did it and he knows a lot about war."

"You are raising just the sorts of issues we hoped for," Mrs. Yingling said.

"Exactly," Mr. Rehlin added.

"Tomorrow," Mr. Enloe said, "we'll come back to school and take on these issues. Niraji said it well—'strange and interesting.' What do we really know and what might people think we know? These are complicated questions."

"Mr. Enloe, my real simple question," Dean said, "is, What do we wear? How dressed up do we have to get?"

"On the radio, Dean," Mia said, "you can wear your birthday suit. No one sees you."

"Oh yes, *you* can!" he countered.

"And we radio persons will wear the sunglasses so not to see you brightly," Junior commented.

"See you tomorrow, folks," Mr. Enloe said with a sense of temporary closure.

2

The First Interviews

At 8:58 A.M. the next morning, Japanese folk music played over the stereo intercom system throughout the school. People began to congregate in the commons. The meeting bell rang twice. It was another day for folding paper peace birds.

"Good morning," Mr. Enloe greeted everyone. "We've got a number of things to do today. We need to work on our questions and determine who is going to do what. We have more information on the number of interviews we've been asked to do as well as specifics on the broadcast. We also need to put together a press kit on the International School."

"I don't understand this *press* and *kit*," Junior said.

"Everyone knows you well, Junior," Curtis commented. "You were on TV last month at the opening of that new Brasil Cafe."

"Being there for my country, of course!" he replied.

"And instant stardom and free coffee," Kino added.

"Okay, quiet please," Mr. Enloe interrupted. "Junior, you know the press are journalists, broadcasters, and newspaper reporters. We give them a kit, which is a package of materials, in this case information on the school, a brochure, a description of our curriculum, and a photograph."

"Thank you," Junior said, grinning.

"Muito bem," everybody chimed in, using Junior's native Portuguese. Each time a new student arrived, the other students learned a few words in the new student's language. Usually these included hello, thank you, good-bye, and one or two words that fell in the "wow," "hip," "cool" category.

"What we will do right now," Mr. Enloe continued, "is to break into four groups, each focused on one of the areas we discussed yesterday. Each group will have a record keeper, and you have two jobs. First, discuss reasonable, clear responses to each question. Second, look up here at the board and note that the category about the A-bomb is empty. From the perspective of your group's category, are there questions and responses you can put under 'A-bomb'? Group leaders for this work will be Christina, 'Living in Hiroshima'; Curtis, 'Japanese People'; Mai, 'Going to School'; and Nicola, 'Personal/School.'

"You've got ninety minutes. Your teachers will come around to offer advice and counsel. Material resources include a copy for each group of 'A Guide to Hiroshima for Foreign Residents, Hiroshima,' published by the mayor's office, old copies of *Hiroshima Signpost*,[3] and the Peace Culture Foundation's *Hiroshima Peace Reader*. Other resources are in the library. Ask us if you need help. Let's go, gang!"

---

3. A monthly culture and local interest magazine published by the school for foreign residents.

The Meaning of It All

While students began to forms groups according to their interests, Mrs. Yingling reviewed the requests for interviews the school had received. *Chugoku Shinbun*, the area's major newspaper, known nationally as a muckraking "peace news paper," wanted to interview several non-American students on Tuesday. RCC television had scheduled a Wednesday morning interview at their studios next to Hiroshima Castle with four or five "Americans" for major U.S. television stations. ("Americans" included anyone foreign. Kids from the United States, Canada, and Australia all planned to be American for the interviews.) European and Australian broadcasters wanted to meet with foreign students Wednesday afternoon at the Hiroshima Peace Culture Foundation regarding the International Kids' Network broadcast. A number of reporters hoped students would be available to be interviewed on Thursday and asked that they be at the press headquarters after the ceremony in Peace Park.

"I think these are all the requests we can fulfill," John Rehlin said.

"John, I even question whether we can do all of this well," Walter commented. "The kids are great, and I know that they can do an excellent job of presenting themselves. My main concern is that we are being asked to take on the role of speaking for the foreign community."

"And even for the world," Steve commented. "To some people, one foreigner represents all foreigners. Anyone from any country who is tagged black or white is seen by many

Japanese as American. Ironic, isn't it, that their ethnocentrism brings races together. They see us as all being alike."

"These venues also mean that all the kids can participate—that is, everybody who wants to," John said. "It would have been hard to choose only one student to be a radio commentator."

"Mayumi," Walter said to Mrs. Yingling, "I want you to know how appreciative we are that you have done everything possible to make sure this is a wonderful learning experience for the children."

"Doitasimashite.[4] I want to avoid what has sometimes happened; the children have been pawns or have become tokens used to 'internationalize' an event. Of course we'll also take our cards of good wishes to the Atomic Bomb Hospital. Serene and Satoshi went there with me several days ago. I took them to help me think about our service projects. We'll make cards in which a crane opens its wings when you open the card. We'll need our usual 150. But then again what is true service? For whom? To whom?"

Mayumi thought for a moment and then commented, "Our children can speak from their hearts and minds about living here and about their feelings and insights about peace and nuclear war."

"Do we give them time to do so? What opportunities do they have?" Walter asked.

"Well, it happens naturally," Mayumi said.

"Perhaps more by happenstance," Walter said.

"We need to feel deeply, watch strongly, and think

---

4. "Don't mention it."

hard—be like water from a deep well—about everything these next weeks," Mayumi continued.

"And to remember the past is to work for the future," commented John.

"You know," Walter said, "I've been here since 1980 and teaching about the bomb or the cold war has never been part of our curriculum. Of course Japanese culture and the students' own cultures are integral to what we do. I agree to sit in the well and find its belly, its center."

"With your belly and its center." By this Mayumi meant that we should contemplate deeply and allow our thoughts and feelings to reveal themselves.

"It will be interesting to see what the kids learn and struggle with and the concerns and questions they generate during the next several days."

Steve said, "I think it's fascinating to consider what questions and responses the kids are coming up with right now."

Lonny commented, "Yes. I know there are some big gaps in their knowledge base and there are many questions for which they have no answers."

"Just like us," Walter added, and the others nodded in agreement. "I like ambiguity. Multiple perspectives are the only soulfully healthy approach to this whole issue—learning to see that there are multiple perspectives on what is assumed to be the same event or idea."

"That's for sure," John said. "And the more I know about Japan, the less I understand."

"I feel the same way about the nuclear question," Walter said.

"Life," John mused. "We're talking about the questions of life and death and the meaning of it all."

Be True to Your School

The moderator at the press interview was Mr. Tashiro, or Tashiro-san, a reporter and a friend of the international community. He and his wife were members of the World Friendship Center and co-translators of *Hiroshima Peace Reader.* At the *Chugoku Shinbun* building the students were ushered into a small auditorium, where they sat at a table with microphones under bright lights. In front of them were some twenty reporters, mostly for Asian newspapers and magazines. Tashiro would translate into Japanese and English. Simultaneous Chinese and Korean translation was also provided.

Tashiro-san began, "If a visitor came to your school, what would he be surprised by?"

Heather spoke first. She was fourteen and had lived in Japan a year. "This school is quite different from my school in Australia. A visitor to our school might be amazed to find the whole group of kids involved and busy at work."

"In a sense it is amazing because it is unusual to find kids, what you say, not goofing off," Johann added.

"It's because people just can't be disinterested," Mia said, "because there is so much to do and we're so small that everybody is needed to be involved."

"Can you give us an example?" a reporter asked.

"Well," Harold said, "last spring we played several basketball games against the junior varsity team from Canadian Academy in Kobe. We all participated. Mai and Heather played on the boys' team and made it co-ed. Everybody went on a trip there and helped out with cheerleading and banners and all of that. Of course we have 100 students. They have

700." Harold's example revealed something of the spirit of cooperation that pervades the school. This, along with respect for others and their cultural heritage, helps make the school a caring and creative place.

"Sometimes it is so lonely living in another culture. Even in Japan, where everybody is so nice, still you are an outsider and everybody knows it." Niraj said. He was twelve years old now and had lived in Japan for four years. The first year he had attended Japanese school, and soon he would return to India.

"Does everybody in your school study Japanese?" Tashiro-san asked.

"Yes, we do," replied Mia. She had been at the school longest, some six years.

"Do you like it and why?"

"Yes, I do," Mia continued. "Most of us like it because it is fun and interesting. Our principal lived in Japan as a boy and he hated to study because it was boring and not very useful. He hired Mrs. Yingling to help make our lessons less boring."

"How so?" Tashiro-san asked.

"We learn conversational Japanese that you can use at a record store or on the bus or at the playground. If you want to study even more, of course you can, and many people do."

"What kinds of things do you study about Japan?"

"We study some Japanese history, and we also learn Japanese songs, both folk and contemporary. Same with dance. We cook; we do arts and crafts, including sumi, origami, and raku pottery, and Mr. Miller works with students to refinish old tansu, wooden boxes and chests, which we sell at our annual bazaar," Mia paused. "What else?"

"We study martial arts—judo, karate, and kendo," said another student.

"We go on field trips all over. We have several camping trips a year. Our favorite is to Miyajima Island," Harold commented.

"We have several sister schools we visit for home stays and our yearly Undokai and Gakugeikai,"[5] Nicole said.

❧ We Run Everything

The students paused for a moment. Then Tashiro-san said, "Well again, what's so special about your school?"

"I'll tell you what," Mia said. "This is the kind of place where the students say to a visitor, 'This is our school; we're in charge. We run everything.'"

"And we do," Heather and Harold said in unison, then laughed and put their hands up to their faces in a gesture of "cool."

One of the reporters asked, "What are you running?"

Harold said, "Well, we have a budget of 750,000 yen a year ($7,250 US) that comes from our drink sales, T-shirt sales, and money from the school budget. We plan our field trips. We organize all the daily school cleanups. We even assign the principal cleanup jobs. And we have weekly meetings where we make decisions."

"We also give away 34 percent of our money. After a lot of research, we chose Children's Defense Fund, because most of their money goes directly to help kids."

"We also make all the school rules," Mia added.

---

5. *Undokai* is a sports day and *Gakugeikai* is a culture festival.

"Well, there are only five or six of them," Johann said.

"What are they?" Tashiro-san inquired.

"The first one is 'Be kind.' 'Live respectfully' is another. Then there are rules about shoes."

"What do you mean?" a reporter asked.

"In our school," Mia said, "each day we have three sets of shoes: the ones we wear outside, our indoor shoes, and our gym shoes. You can't wear the gym shoes in the hall or outside or your outside shoes in or your inside shoes outside. It keeps the school clean. I know because this summer I'm in charge of the upstairs halls."

"Other rules are about gum and caffeine drinks," Harold put in. "A couple of years ago the older students realized that chewing gum and caffeine drinks are unsuitable for school. So we made a rule about it. And the adults had to stop their coffee and tea drinking during school hours."

"How did they behave about this?" Tashiro-san asked.

"Well, they did it, because the rules are the same for everybody at the school. It was an okay rule," Harold said, "because it was made by the whole school."

❧ The Students and Japan

"What do you like about Japan?" a reporter asked.

"I like the people and food and places to go," Mia said.

"Me too," Heather said. "But mostly I like the International School. I've gone to schools in London, Detroit, and Australia, and this is the best."

"I like this school too," Niraj said. "Many students are world travelers and have lived in several countries and speak two or more languages. We all study English and Japanese every day and also our home language. I study Hindi at school by special course through the mail to my home school teacher."

"So do I," Johann said. He had previously lived in Bombay, India, where his father worked as an architect for a Swedish shipbuilding firm. "I really like it that all the people are friendly. There are not any—what you say, Mia—ah clichés?"

"Cliques," Mia said.

"Right," Johann continued. "Everybody gets along here. It doesn't matter where you from, what you speak, your parents' job."

"Being a girl does matter though," Heather jumped in. "Being immature ones—these boys here—does matter too."

"Yes, your majesty," Harold intoned, bowing toward her.

"What's your favorite quotation by your hero, Niraj?" Mia asked him.

"Judge a person by the content of his character and not by the color of his skin," Niraj recalled effortlessly. "Doctor Martin Luther King Junior."

"It's true here," Harold said, "at the school. But you still are a gaijin on the streets and at the playgrounds."

"And everywhere else," Johann added.

"What is it that bothers you about the word *gaijin*?" Tashiro asked.

For a moment no one said anything, and the students just looked at each other. Then Mia spoke. "The polite form is gaikokujin, not gaijin."

"It's a label. 'Outsider' is so inconsiderate," Heather said.

"It's like you're a barbarian," Mai added. "Who needs to be labeled?"

"Even in schools," Isaac added. "Being labeled 'gifted' is as dangerous as being labeled 'handicapped' or 'disabled.'"

"I'm used to it," Johann said. "What I don't like is being labeled American just because I'm other than the Japanese."

"I hate being called black," Nicole said. "I want to be me. Look at my family. The stupid thing is that if your mother is white and your dad black or the other way around, you're labeled black, not white, not mixed." Nicole was from Vancouver. Her parents were cancer researchers. They were both born in Trinidad and were now Canadian citizens. Nicole had dual citizenship.

"Jap or Japanese? They both stink," Mai said.

"Negro or nigger? They both hurt," Nicole joined in.

"Gaijin is liked being called 'nigger' or 'Jap' or 'Chink' or whatever," Junior said. "In Brazil most of us are mixed."

"Hey so are we," Isaac said. "I mean who knows anything about their great-great-great-grandfather's great-grandmother? We're all combinations of people mixed up. What is white really? Someday maybe we'll not be color-blind but colorless. From multicultural to intercultural."

"In a thousand years maybe. Look, am I Japanese New Zealander or New Zealander Japanese?" Kino asked. "Maybe Japlander."

"You are a mixooh uptoh boy," Isaac commented.

"Me too," Johann said. "Am I German Dutch or Dutch German?"

"Dutchman," Kino said.

"I don't like it either," Heather said.

"You are a girl in the moon?" Junior asked.

"Look back in the past. What do you see?" Heather asked.

"Adam and Eve?" Isaac said.

"Racism," Mai said.

"Ethnocentrism," Niraj said.

"It's right here, hear me!" Nicole yelled.

Niraj added, "I'm not white or black. I'm me!"

"It's really true—we don't label each other and we don't tolerate people labeling others," Mia said. "I do get labeled 'mixed.' I see myself as both or double."

"Right. I'm mixed too," added Harold, who was half Dutch and one-fourth each Indonesian and Guyanan. "We use the word Japanese instead of Jap or Nip. That's really the difference we feel with gaikokujin and gaijin."

"It's too bad. So sad," Johann said.

"In America if your mother is black and your father white, you are categorized as black! Sooo dumb!" Nicole repeated.

"It started a long time ago. And it's still here," Harold added.

"Isn't it right now too?" Niraj asked. "Isn't it all connected, this racism, ethnocentrism, sexism, nuclearism?"

"Nuclearism?" Mai asked.

"I made that one up," said Niraj.

"Don't forget my dad's number one word for teachers—adultocentrism," Isaac added.

"Nuclearism. We should get rid of all the bombs," Mia continued, "but I don't really know a lot about it."

"Big fortieth!" Harold said. "Will you reporters come back next year? No one was asking us questions last summer. Or will you come back on the fiftieth?"

City of Peace

Tashiro said, "This is the International City of Peace and Culture. How is that so?"

"Because they say it is," Niraj said.

"Who?" Harold inquired.

"The peoples in the government, the people who make the signs and brochures." Niraj said. "My father said it is a huge issue, this nuclear position, because even in Japan there are many viewpoints."

"War is bad news," Mia commented.

"It is the Peace City, but do people in other parts of Japan know? I don't even know it until now," Niraj said.

"What does Hiroshima mean to you? One word or two, please. Your first thoughts," Tashiro-san asked as a final question.

"Nice people," Harold said.

"Wide islands," Niraj added.

"Venice of East," Heather said reading from her brochure comparing the "water cities."

"Beautiful beaches and views of the Inland Sea," Junior added, reading from Heather's brochure.

"Peace City," Johann said. He had wanted to say, "Not one of the sixteen or nineteen Nuclear Free Cities in Japan." His older brother, Anders, who was studying in Switzerland at boarding school, had made him promise on the phone last night he would say that, but Johann wasn't sure. For one thing, he didn't know if it was true. And second, he wasn't really sure what a nuclear free zone was.

And that was the end of the interview. It had been enjoyable and interesting but somewhat disconcerting. As Heather and Johann thought about the questions they had been asked, they reflected out loud. "I don't really know very much about Hiroshima," said Heather. "I live here and I like it, but I don't know much."

"I'm the same," said Johann. "I know little about the A-bomb. Or World War II. Nothing really at all, you know." He thought, that's going change. I'm going to find out more; maybe I'll find even more than I want to know right now.

Tashiro-san made sure that the reporters got their names, ages, and country and number of years in Japan: Nicole, 13, Trindad and Canada, two years; Mia, 12, Canada, six years; Heather, 14, Australia, one year; Junior, 14, Brazil, one year; Niraji, 12, India, three years; Harold, 13, Holland, two years; Johann, 13, Sweden, three years; and so on. Tashiro-san gave them each a booklet and a T-shirt commemorating the fortieth anniversary of the atomic bombing, a print of a dove sitting on top of the peace dome with the words No More Hiroshimas emblazoned across the bottom. The T-shirts were all the same size, too small for everyone but Niraj and Mia.

The students split up and rode back to school. Mia, Heather, and few others decided to walk home. They stopped at a small coffee shop near Heather's apartment and had ice cream.

"That was interesting and a bit strange," Mia said as she flipped through the booklet *Hiroshima: 40 Years, Never to Forget the Future*.

"I know. Why were we interviewed? I don't get it," Johann exclaimed.

"They need a story. Our living here is something different," Harold replied.

"But I don't see much of a connection with it and the peace ceremony and the commemoration week." Johann was frustrated.

"We didn't need to be on stage with the lights and all," Mia said.

"Everybody gets to be famous for fifteen minutes, Mrs. Yingling says," Niraj added.

"That soup can artist Andy Warhol got more than fifteen. How about a year?" Harold said.

"Well, we get at least twenty," Mia said.

"Look, this booklet's got some spelling errors. They should have to be in Mr. Mudge's language arts class," Heather suggested.

"It's the message that counts anyway, isn't it?" Mia commented.

"Look at this title. It's strange. I can't figure this place out," Johann said.

"Remember, when you can't figure out Japanese, say Mr. Rehlin's motto," Mia smiled.

"The more you know, the less you understand," they sang out in unison.

3

Nuclear Nightmares

It was the afternoon before "A-bomb day," as Dean announced. Dean, Isaac, Yuri, and Janelle had been selected to be interviewed. Yuri, who was from Detroit, had lived in Japan for several years. Both of her parents were engineers for Ford and were first-generation Korean-Americans. Yuri, who in her words, "looked Japanese but felt American," was the first to volunteer for this interview with American students.

Yuri was "as American as a cheeseburger," but she often experienced discrimination because Japanese kids either thought she was a Japanese student who was "stupid" because she couldn't speak Japanese or they knew her family was from Korea, Japan's enemy for hundreds of years.

Isaac had lived in Japan the longest of the three. This was his sixth year in Japan and his fourth year at the International School. He went to Japanese School two years, studied karate in a Buddhist temple, and spoke fluent Japanese. Despite his blue eyes and blond hair, people thought he was Japanese, especially if they were hearing him on the phone. He thought he was "both or double"—bilingual and bicultural. His friend Dean was two weeks older than he was and was also from his hometown of Atlanta, Georgia, where their parents had been friends since high school. Walter, Elizabeth, and Steve had first met as teenagers in Japan when their parents (Dean's and Isaac's grandparents) were teaching there. Dean was also fluent in Japanese and had gone to Japanese school for three years. Isaac and Dean were fascinated by the notion that the press might think of the A-bomb as both the atomic and the American bomb. Many Japanese people did.

Janelle's hometown was Seattle and she had been in Japan for less than six months, the past term only. For her, Hiroshima and Japan were still new and different. She was comfortable with her family and school friends, but the real Japan was in between her home and the island. Sometimes she sat on a bench in the middle of a park or along the street and just watched and listened to the real Japan.

Mr. Enloe accompanied the three to the interview sessions, where he was to be interviewed by a television crew from Atlanta. Walter had lived in Hiroshima twenty years earlier when he was in grades seven through nine. He didn't attend the International School with his sisters, because it took students only through grade six. Instead, he traveled two hours by bus to Iwakuni, where a United States naval air station was home to a small high school of some forty American students. Walter wondered if the reporters thought he had some insights into Hiroshima because he had lived there as both a teenager and a adult. He wasn't sure that he did.

❧ The Second Interview

The interview began innocuously enough, following closely the format of the previous day's international interview.

Reporters had come from the United States, Canada, England, Sweden, Australia, New Zealand, India, Germany, France and Japan. The first questions were of the "Who are you and what do you do?" variety. The students felt well prepared.

Then the young reporter from Atlanta, Katherine Louise, spoke. She noted that her questions grew out of her interviews the past few days with Hiroshima residents, including Japanese bomb victims and American sojourners.

"What kinds of Hiroshima dreams do you have?" she asked. The room was silent.

"Who wants to go first?" she prodded.

The students looked at each other and shrugged.

"We understand some American children have nuclear nightmares."

It was still so quiet you could hear the cameras whirring and the audience breathing. The microphones seemed to pick up the silent speaking in Yuri and Dean and Isaac's and Janelle's eyes as well as the beating of their hearts.

Still there was a crescendo of silence. The reporter looked at Mr. Enloe. He said nothing. Who had she talked to? he thought. He tried to imagine who might know American kids well enough to say they had dreams of nuclear mass destruction.

Finally Katherine Louise said, "I guess I'm trying to ask if you ever get scared here."

"I go anywhere I want in Hiroshima," Isaac said. "On my bike and the trolleys, I explore and play all around the city with my friends. I've never been scared of Hiroshima."

"The first weeks I was here we went on a field trip into the mountains to our sister school to spend the day," Janelle said. "I was afraid at first when I was in a group of Japanese kids by myself and couldn't say anything at all in Japanese."

"The same for me," Dean said. "I started Japanese school not knowing a thing except 'sushi' and 'karate.' At least my brother, Yoshi, looked Japanese. He is half and is adopted. I stood out."

"Did anyone try to hurt you?" the reporter asked.

"Not really. The boys would roughhouse and bully you unless you stood up to them. The teachers were nice and most kids were really friendly or just left you alone."

"But kids, how is it living here in the first city destroyed by an atomic bomb? Aren't you afraid of the nuclear radiation?"

"I haven't ever really thought about it," Isaac said. "I've never heard people talk or worry about it since I came here."

"Well, you read about peoples' fears of radiation poisoning, people dying from radiation cancers, mutations, nothing able to grow for years," Katherine said.

"Long ago or science fiction," Mr. Enloe commented from the shadows.

"My parents are both doctors at the Radiation Effects Research Foundation. My mom's a radiologist and my dad's a biostatistician," Janelle said. "I know we wouldn't live here if it wasn't safe."

"Same here," Dean agreed.

"Do you really feel safe? We understand many hibakusha silently resent Americans living in Hiroshima," Katherine continued.

"What do you mean they resent us?" Isaac asked. The other kids also spoke up.

"They don't like Americans living here?" Dean asked.

"Really?" said Janelle.

"Who said?" Dean asked.

"That's what we were told," replied Katherine.

"I don't agree," Isaac said.

"No one has treated me badly because of the bomb," Dean said.

"Me either," Isaac said. "But when my dad was a kid, things were different. Right, dad?"

"Some," said Walter. "I'll speak about it when it's my turn."

"Okay," Katherine continued. "Do you feel guilty for what happened?"

"What do you mean?" Isaac asked.

"The bombing forty years ago tomorrow," she replied.

"I wasn't alive," Janelle remarked.

"I wasn't there," Dean said.

"My parents were not even there," Janelle added.

"Don't you feel guilty because you are an American?" Katherine asked.

"I'm not sure," Isaac said. "And how does it relate to Pearl Harbor, if it does?"

"That's a point," Dean said. "And how about the Japanese trying to build a bomb?"

"I don't feel guilty. I'm sorry it happened," Janelle stated.

"It was a war and Japan helped start it," Isaac added.

"Should we think of the atomic bomb as a different kind of war?" asked the reporter.

"I don't know," Janelle pondered.

"Me either," Yuri said quietly.

"Who's at fault in all this?" Mia whispered. "Us? Or the adults?"

This set of questions seemed to conclude the interview. The students stood up and left the table in silence.

❧ Twenty Years Earlier

Now it was Mr. Enloe's turn. The students stood in the shadows of the stage and lights. Walter addressed the reporters: "I don't know what questions you plan to ask, but I hope they aren't as difficult as the ones you just asked my students. I mean, wow, who have you been talking to? Hiroshima is in our dreams and waking moments, too. But to suggest that most kids and perhaps adults are dreaming nightmares of Hiroshima—well, it is not part of my experience. Perhaps it should be, but it isn't."

"We weren't going to ask you exactly the same questions, but they might be similar," a reporter said. The first question was straightforward.

"When did you first move to Hiroshima?" A reporter pointed her mike at him.

"I moved at age twelve in 1961 to Japan and in 1963 to Hiroshima, and I lived here until 1966," replied Walter.

"Why did you move here?" she asked.

"My parents captured me in Atlanta and forced me to move here! Actually, they worked for a Protestant church as a minister and a teacher, and they have lived in Japan for almost thirty years."

"Still?"

"Yes. They're right down the road in Saka, outside Kure, on the Inland Sea."

"Maybe we should speak with them."

"They wouldn't want to. There is too much in the

present and the future of their lives and work. Their attitude is rather Japanese: Move on. Respect the past, even fear it, but don't dwell there."

"What was living here like twenty years ago?"

"It could be a hundred years, two hundred, and it wouldn't make a difference where the differing begins." Walter paused and focused on his children—his students and his son. Their eyes beckoned and seemed to pull him.

"When I was thirteen years old, we lived near Hiroshima University, and I spent a lot of time after school and on weekends on the campus. Many people who were students or teachers at the time remember the American kid hanging around the sports field and gym. I was befriended by many students, but most people simply left me alone.

"My real friends were my brother and four Japanese kids who were our age. Kenji was two years older than I, and we spoke only Japanese. His father had a plumbing business, and Kenji rode a 250cc Honda Scrambler that belonged to his older brother. We traveled to the city at least once a week from the mountains to downtown, to Peace Park, to Miyajima Island. We ate at each other's homes.

"Keiko and Kato lived within fifty yards of us on a side street, off the major intersection and trolley strop at Hiroshima University and the Red Cross (and atomic bomb) Hospital. Kato's father was a day laborer and his mother was a cleaning woman. He and his sister and parents lived in a one-room apartment that was about fifteen meters square. The bathroom was down the hall.

"Kato was a good student who studied hard. His parents rented a small room that was big enough for Kato and his sister to use as a study room. He studied about five or six hours a night. We played ball together, and we often met at night for ice cream or a soda at Keiko's parents' store, which was two doors down from my house. We spoke Nihongrish —mixed English and Japanese. When we first became friends we each had pocket dictionaries.

"Now that I think about it, I realize that I developed friendships with fellow students right there on my street within fifty meters of each other—nothing special, just natural. I think that say a lot about the times back then, doesn't it?" He continued, "The war was over, though the bombing lingered in the hearts and minds of people. Still, I was not ostracized and made friends with neighbors; even if people didn't like you or even hated you they were civil. People might be bowing politely to you and inside saying 'I hate gaijin,' but in my experience only one in about ten thousand felt that way."

Walter paused and the room was silent for a moment except for the mechanical whirring of cameras. "And Keiko?" someone asked.

"My first girl friend, a person I became good friends with, just friends. I spoke mostly English with her. She later became a Japan Airlines Stewardess—because of my English lessons, she said."

"What kinds of things did you talk about?"

"Life, experiencing, communicating, understanding, exploring, laughter!" Walter exclaimed. "We talked of friendship and love."

"And not once," he continued, "did we talk about the bomb. Ever. Even when we hung out in Peace Park, we didn't talk about the bomb. Our talk was about music, movies, our studies, but never the bomb or radiation or even peace."

"Even when you stood at the children's monument or the cenotaph?"

"The first time I was there I felt serenity as well as a great sense of sadness and death. When you look intently from the cenotaph through the eternal flame and the somber atom-bomb dome, you see the walls and lights of the Hiroshima Carp baseball stadium. This juxtaposition of sadness and playfulness, of the past and the present joined, is very strange and prevalent in this place we know as Hiroshima."

"Twenty years ago were foreigners treated differently?"

"Well, there were very few foreigners. I'd ride my bike downtown through the Hondori and not see another foreigner. Now I'd see ten or twenty. The International School had twenty or thirty students at most. But my friendships were very strong then, as strong as today with Japanese peers.

"Only once was I verbally abused by an older man on a trolley. One side of his face was a keloid scar, so he was probably hibakusha. He kept talking loudly about the bad Americans, how stupid we are and how we have hurt Japan. No one said anything. I tried not to look at him. I could tell other people were annoyed, but they really didn't know what to do. I was about fourteen, and I kept thinking, Why blame me? Why treat me as if I represented America or the military.

"This must have been in 1963 or 1964, around the time when there was a great debate in Japan about its defense treaty with the United States. I remember many demonstrations in front of the Iwakuni base by antiwar and anti-defense-treaty protesters. Also at this time, Americans living on the military base were forbidden to visit Hiroshima. Even though I went to school there every day, none of my friends could come home with me. That was weird."

"What else do you remember from your early years in Hiroshima?"

"Well, I was a tutor; that is, I spoke English each week with an economics professor who later became academic dean of Hiroshima University. Through him I was invited to join the English Speaking Society (ESS), a group on campus. I went to their meetings sometimes. Most of them were excellent speakers of English. Everybody begins studying English in the seventh grade. By the end of high school their reading ability in English is phenomenal. But there was little time spent speaking English, except in ESS clubs. I do remember one time when the topic was U.S.–Japanese relations and the discussion became very heated. I felt myself asking, Am I to blame just because I was born in the United States?"

"And how about Roy?"

"He was my brother's friend. He lived next door and was probably five to seven years older than we were. I think his name was Kenji, but he called himself Roy. His father owned movie theaters and he wanted to be a movie director. Once I had a bit role with several of my friends in a film called *Umi no Wakadaisho*, and Roy acted if I were a famous star. In the film we didn't say a word; we played roles of swimmers on an Australian university team in Japan for an international meet. I was on film maybe for three minutes. But the star of the film was as popular as Elvis. Kayama Yuzo was a big star of young adult adventure romance movies and leader of the rock group The Spiders. If Elvis did *Blue Hawaii*, Kayama Yuzo would do *Red Kyoto*. I signed hundreds of autographs, usually a variation of James Dean, because of that film.

"Roy made a short film about us living in Hiroshima, and my mother still has a copy. Roy and my brother really got along. But I felt he liked me only because I was an American friend he could show off to his friends."

"What stands out after all those years in Hiroshima?"

"I've given you a sense of the light and gray sides, but what about the dark side?" Walter closed his eyes and slowly, quietly began to put words to a flow of emotion: "Alone ...silence...one of them...the perpetrators... penance ...Ugly American...guilt by association...hiding inwardly and silently ...their eyes...he's one of them that did that to us...in all of their eyes and in the mind's eye, wasn't I one of them?"

"I read so many different perspectives." Tashiro-san noted.

"What I do know is the story my father tells of when we moved to Hiroshima in the early sixties. We began going to Dr. Morita, a local dentist. He had studied in Germany and spoke English too. He was probably seventy years old at the time. Each time we would go to his house where he had his office, we would sit in his living room and drink green tea and eat little cookies filled with red bean paste. And we would talk. Then we would brush our teeth and he would fill our cavities or do whatever needed to be done. Afterward we would go into his garden and inspect the many varieties of roses he was cultivating. Going to his home was a wonderful experience.

"One winter my father invited Dr. Morita to a Christmas party at a local church. On the way home, as they were talking, the subject of war and the atomic bombing came up. My dad talked about serving in the U.S. Marine Air Corps on Iwo Jima and Guam, and Dr. Morita told of serving the local population through the Japanese Imperial Medical Corps. Then they talked about the day of the bombing. Dr. Morita said his home was not destroyed as it was some distance from the center of town, but his only son, a thirteen-year-old junior high student, was riding a trolley to school when it was incinerated.

"My father's heart stopped when he heard this. How could this devout Buddhist dentist who had lost his only son in a war with the United States in the most horrific of deaths show such genuine affection and goodwill to his American friends? And here was my father, a minister who years earlier as a young soldier had been taught to despise the Japanese as an enemy who was called 'cold-blooded' and 'yellow vermin.' My dad, Isaac's grandfather, as a young soldier lost many friends to Japanese bombs and guns. And now here he was in Hiroshima building friendships with people he had been taught to hate."

❧ Searching for Closure

"What have been the greatest changes you've noticed in Hiroshima?"

"Well, the city has grown tremendously. It's worked hard to become both a beautiful city and the International City of Peace and Culture, including supporting its International School. Five years ago, if I had arrived at Hiroshima Station and asked a taxi driver to take me to the International School, he would have been dumbfounded. If I had said 'American School,' I'd be there in minutes. Today everyone knows that Hiroshima has an International School."

"Well, thank you very much, all of you," said one of the reporters, drawing the session to a close. The interviews were now formally over, but the conversation continued.

"Your questions to our students were a bit disconcerting," Walter told Tashiro-san, "I can't answer them myself."

"It must be difficult, yes," she said. "I have another question for you."

"Sure," he said.

"Did you ever worry about radiation levels or about getting radiation sickness when you were a child in Hiroshima?"

"Somewhat," replied Walter.

"In what ways?" asked the reporter.

"When we found out we were moving to Hiroshima, my uncle in Mississippi, who had been a U.S. Army paratrooper and had been trained, if it is possible, for nuclear war, sent me a birthday card. On it he had written a note that said, 'Don't drink the water; don't eat the fish. Radioactivity lives for 80,000 years.' I was a bit spooked."

"Yes," said the reporter, indicating she was expecting more.

"My dad told us not to fear anything, though he warned us not to eat food from small stalls on the street, since the vendors didn't use soap to wash their dishes and utensils. But his main point was that 450,000 people were living in Hiroshima and so would we."

"Did you have any other concerns?" Tashiro-san asked.

"Well, we moved to Hiroshima some months after the 1962 Cuban missile crisis, and I remember thinking that if the whole world blew up, then that was that. But for the first time I thought living in Hiroshima was better than living in Atlanta, which was not that far from Cuba. Lightning didn't strike twice in the same place time, and I assumed that neither did nuclear bombs. Pretty naive? Big time!"

"Did you think about the bombing?" asked the reporter.

"Well sure, not every day, but sometimes I saw scarred people or I thought about the Red Cross Hospital across from my home or I read about nuclear warfare talks with the Russians. I had dreams, not nightmares, but dreams that seemed to mollify those conscious anxieties and the unconscious fears of living in the Nuclear Age. Certainly I was impressionable—I remember playing nuclear war and bomb shelter games in Atlanta; one day Davy Crockett and the next atomic war." Walter paused and thought for a moment and then continued, "Some of my family members have cancer, and the previous generation did not. So I don't know. The years we lived in this environment, in Hiroshima, drinking the water, eating the food, kicking up dirt as we played...I don't really know if there is a connection..."

"Any regrets about living here?"

"None. In fact I wish I had lived here earlier."

"Why?"

"Because I would be even more a son of Hiroshima than I am after fifteen years of living in Japan."

"What do you Americans living in Hiroshima do to contribute to peace?"

"Wait a second, please; let's ask my students. Kids, come over and join me," Mr. Enloe called to the students, and to the reporter he said, "Ask them. They know."

"Students, what do Americans living in Hiroshima do to contribute to peace?"

Isaac answered immediately, "We have a peaceful school, we all get along, the older kids help the younger kids, and we raise money for our trips and donate a third of it to UNESCO programs and to the Children's Defense Fund. We also have a conflict resolution program that everybody participates in."

"But what about peace in Hiroshima? What do you do for the peace movement?" the reporter asked.

"We live here," Dean said. "Isn't that enough?"

SOON AFTER THAT, as the students were leaving the television station, Yuri said, "Well that was strange—almost like she wanted to put words in our mouths."

"Exactly how I felt, too," Isaac said.

"She seemed to think she knows the truth, and yet I'm not convinced she understands people's true feelings," Mr. Enloe said.

As a car drove up, Dean said, "I gotta go. There's my mom. Do you want a ride, Yuri?"

"Sure," she replied. "See you tomorrow," Yuri called to the others.

"Bye."

"Bye."

Isaac and his dad walked along the canal from the TV station past Hiroshima Castle, the original target of the bombing. The castle's roof cast dark images along the towering walls onto the street. Walter and Isaac passed through the shadows, talking little. Both were consumed by the past hours and days, immersed in the ambiguities and paradoxes of this place called Hiroshima. They walked past Nobori Junior High School and soon arrived home. Isaac called Dean, who agreed to meet at seven the next morning at the temple next to Shukkien Gardens. From there they would bike to Peace Park. Then it was time to retire for the evening. The day had been intense, and tomorrow would be nearly as challenging.

❧ 4

Peace Park Ceremony

The next morning, students gathered at the children's monument in Peace Park by 7:30. Dean and Isaac rode their bikes; Nicole and Christina came by bus; Mai took a taxi. From there they went to the radio broadcast booth and took their seats. From the booth they could see the whole spectacle of peacemaking and remembrance.

Thousands of people were gathering. The children's monument was a central location from which to witness the coming together of people throughout the world to commemorate the day. Turning south, the students could see the eternal flame and the sacred pool and behind it the saddle-shaped cenotaph. In the foreground was the museum, and in front of it on a thousand chairs sat the invited guests, all wearing ribbons of red and white. The mayor and other dignitaries were surrounded by tens of thousands of flowers. The mayor walked to the podium decked in black bunting. Thousands stood throughout the park, ringing the solemn area. At 8:16 the bells tolled. Hundreds of doves lifted in a beautiful stream of white, and like a trail of smoke in the wind, rose higher and disappeared.

Isaac began to read from his copy of the script: "The mayor of Hiroshima, Mr. Araki, is about to read the Peace Declaration on this fortieth anniversary of the bombing of Hiroshima and the beginning of the Nuclear Age. The mayor stands at the podium, which is covered with thousands of oleander flowers, the flowers that were the first to bloom in Hiroshima after the bombing forty years ago. The bells fade in the background. The mayor bows to the audience of some fifty thousand and begins the incantation:

No More Hiroshimas. It was forty years ago today during the hot summer that the heat waves, fiery blast, and radiation emitted by the first nuclear weapon ever used against a human target burned all living things in a blinding flash and turned the city of Hiroshima into a plain of scorched rubble.

Standing in the ruins, we, the citizens of Hiroshima, foresaw that any war fought with nuclear weapons would mean the annihilation of humanity and the end of civilization, and we have consistently appealed to the world for the total abolition of nuclear weapons.

There was silence. Then Mai began to read as the mayor continued,

Despite these untiring efforts, more and more nuclear weapons have been produced; they have been made more and more sophisticated; and they have been deployed, ready for strategic and tactical use. Humankind continues to face the threat of nuclear annihilation.

Although the nuclear superpowers, the United States and the Soviet Union, finally resumed their long-suspended negotiations on nuclear disarmament this March, the talks have made deplorably little progress as the superpowers use the

facade of negotiation to jockey for advantage while they expand the nuclear arms race into outer space.

Again there was silence, broken gently by a cough, a distant horn, and the sound of a faraway aircraft. Then Kino continued the reading of the mayor's declaration:

Today's hesitation leads to tomorrow's destruction.

"The mayor stops and looks out over the assembled participants," Kino commented, "and repeats his last point,

Today's hesitation leads to tomorrow's destruction.

Then he continues:

In order that Hiroshima's inferno never be repeated anywhere, we strongly urge the United States and the Soviet Union, who hold the fate of humankind in their hands, to halt all nuclear testing immediately and to take decisive steps at the summit talks in Geneva toward the total abolition of nuclear weapons in the interests of all humankind.

As the only country to have experienced nuclear devastation, Japan and the government of Japan should steadfastly adhere to their three non-nuclear principles policy and should take the initiative in seeking the elimination of nuclear weapons. A census on A-bomb victims is being conducted this year, and it is our sincere hope that all due measures will be taken to mitigate the suffering of A-bomb survivors on the basis of the principle of national indemnity, taking into consideration the distinctive characteristics of ailments induced by the atomic bombing.

Effortlessly Christina took over the English narration and began to read the translation as the mayor continued,

Along with these efforts, Hiroshima, an A-bombed city, has devoted itself to building a city dedicated to peace—a living symbol of the ideal of lasting peace. In this spirit we

are hosting the First World Conference of Mayors for Peace through Inter-City Solidarity this year, for it is our hope that all the cities of the world aspiring to lasting peace will be able to develop inter-city solidarity, transcending national boundaries, ideologies, and creeds, and will impart momentum to the international quest for peace.

This year also marks the International Youth Year. We hope that the young people of the world—the leaders of the twenty-first century—will inherit the spirit of Hiroshima, strengthen friendship and solidarity among themselves, and exert their utmost efforts in the cause of peace.

Nicola then continued to read the English narration, following step by step with the mayor.

The fates of all of us are bound together here on earth. There can be no survival for any without peaceful co-existence for all. Humankind has no future if that future does not include co-prosperity. To save this verdant planet from the grim death of nuclear winter, we must draw upon our common wisdom in overcoming distrust and confrontation. Sharing our planet's finite resources in the spirit of mutual understanding and cooperation, we must eliminate starvation and poverty.

Again the mayor paused and looked out over the crowd. Isaac took over the narration:

No more Hiroshimas. We must strengthen the bonds of friendship and solidarity among all peoples so as to save the world from the evil of war. Today, on the occasion of the fortieth anniversary of the atomic bombing of Hiroshima, we pray for the souls of the A-bomb victims and rededicate our lives to the eradication of nuclear weapons and the pursuit of lasting peace.

"Tekeshi Araki, Mayor of Hiroshima, steps back from the podium. Somber music begins as the choir of some hundreds of voices sings, 'This is our cry. This is our prayer. To bring peace into the world.' And as the choir sings, a hundred doves are released in a beautiful display of peaceful flight.

"This is the end of our broadcast from Hiroshima's Peace Park. The International Kids Radio Network is proud to bring you the commemoration ceremony from Hiroshima. At the base of the children's monument in Peace Park, covered in thousands of paper cranes, symbolizing peace, there is an inscription: 'This is our cry. This is our prayer. To bring peace to the world.' That is Hiroshima's message to the world. Good day."

The students were silent for a moment, at once exhausted and exhilarated. Being on stage, even if your audience is invisible, takes a lot of effort.The kids felt like they were pros.

"Well done," Mr. Tashiro exclaimed. "It was a wonderful program."

"Excellent," Mr. Enloe added. "A short and yet poignant ceremony. Your readings were exemplary."

"Congratulations" also came from several of the adults at the radio station and the mayor's office. Mr. Watanabe from the Peace Culture Foundation, which had organized the day's events, gave them each a ceremonial ribbon and a photograph of Peace Park.

At 9:15 all the students who came to the peace ceremony gathered at the benches next to the Children's Monument. It was festooned with a million cranes made from every imaginable folding material from wrapping paper to gum wrappers. Mr. Enloe and Mr. Wiig thanked everyone for coming and asked that over the next few hours they meet other people who were at the park, particularly students and foreign visitors. They also invited everyone to join a group leaving the next day for the Nagasaki Peace Ceremony. The students went off in groups, and Mr. Enloe left for a meeting at the Peace Cultural Foundation. He had the germ of an idea, and he wanted to speak with Ms. Matsubara, who was a librarian at the foundation and a spokesperson worldwide for the hibakusha. She, too, was hibakusha.

Making Peace

Isaac and Dean rode off toward the Hondori, the two-kilometer covered street west of Peace Park that began at the epicenter of the bombing site. At that site originally had stood a private hospital before it was turned to ash and molten rock. Janelle and Yuri went to the International Prayer Ceremony, at which religious leaders from many faiths gathered to sing and pray for peace. Yuri was given a feather by a Native American medicine man from the Crane Clan of the Chippewa from Wisconsin.

Kino and Curtis and Christina went to the area under the Peace Museum that sat some twenty feet off the ground. There Japanese high school students gathered to talk and sing and dance to the rock-and-roll tunes of the fifties and sixties. Two U.S. marines from the Iwakuni military base some forty kilometers away were skateboarding under the museum. Both had burr haircuts; one wore a cape that looked like the U.S. flag. They hung out with Japanese soulmates who sported burr cuts in hues of pink, green, and orange. The atmosphere was a bit like a carnival.

The students had decided to interview the skateboarders and learned that Reggie, from Washington, D.C., was twenty-one and had been a marine for eighteen months. James, nineteen, was from Pigeon Forge, Tennessee. Both were in the service to see the world and learn a job skill, and, as they pointed out, they could earn money for school. They called themselves "two of a few good men." They liked coming to Hiroshima to hang out. What did they think of the significance of Hiroshima?

"The A-bombed city, man," one said.

"Got the big one," the other added.

They talked of their Japanese friends as well as the fact that they couldn't wait to get back home. Neither of them had been inside the museum and didn't plan on going in. That was the past, Reggie said. The future is to be protected by the "biggest, meanest fighting machine in the world."

"We're just keeping the peace," James added and as he skated away, the students could see the large white skull on the back of his black leather jacket.

AT THE PICNIC AREA south of the museum a group of senior high students from some of Hiroshima's sister cities—Honolulu, Dresden, and Volgograd—had gathered with Hiroshima students. Mrs. Yingling had invited Mai and Kino and Janelle and Yuri to attend. She was there with her son, Hideki, or "Eric," who was a senior at the school attached to Hiroshima University. While the food was decidedly Japanese, with *bento,* or wooden lunch boxes of vegetables, fruit, fish, and sushi, the conversation was international.

The Japanese students all read and to some degree spoke English. Some of the students from Honolulu spoke Japanese and some of the Russian and German students spoke English. One student from Hawai'i spoke German. But it was the nonverbal communication, the delightful mix of gestures and facial expressions, that really spoke. Here you could see how a smile was worth a thousand words. There was a bonding of young people as they overcame the barriers of language and culture and politics to enjoy food and friendship and laughter. After lunch the group formed a circle of some fifty people to do folk dancing, first a Russian dance, then a German dance, and then a traditional Japanese dance of the Hiroshima summer festival. There were even some wild attempts at hula dancing.

While some students attended the picnic, Harold and Johann went to interview Mr. Vusamazxula Credo Mutwa from Soweto, South Africa. This was his third visit to Hiroshima and Nagasaki. He was a "witch doctor." Just as Mr. Rehlin had said, he wore an African dashiki, and around his neck he wore the largest necklace anyone had ever seen. It was a heavy, beaten brass yoke, and from the collarbone area hung two carved wooden masks, one of Father Sun and one of Sister Moon. From their mouths came chains linked to a large cross that fell to his belly. And in the middle of Mr. Mutwa's chest hung an emerald green stone in the shape of a human heart.

Mai and Heather wanted to talk with a group of American kids from Seattle who were part of the Children's Peace Choir. Everyone else seemed to be heading off to McDonald's for "flies and hambugoo." The golden arches were glowing in the shadows of the Hiroshima Dome, the only building left to memorialize the destruction of Hiroshima. Mr. Mutwa walked with Harold and Johann to McDonald's and waited outside while they bought burgers. He was a vegetarian, and he asked only for a glass of water.

"I was standing at the cenotaph," he said, "and a Japanese colleague translated the words on the tomb of all those souls who have perished." It was quiet as they sat outside, listening and eating.

"Do you know what it says?" he asked. The students shook their heads.

"It reads: Let all souls here rest in peace, for we shall not repeat the evil." They were quiet for a moment.

"Who do you think 'we' is?" Harold asked.

"Maybe all of us," Johann said. "I don't think it means only Japanese or Americans. You know, the Germans and Japanese both had tried to build an atomic bomb, and they would have used it, I'm sure."

"I think you're right young man—it's all of us," said the doctor. "We need such a monument in South Africa for apartheid and all those who have died. You know, we're still not free."

"What do you mean?" Dean asked.

"In our country we have a system of forced separation, where the white minority controls the black majority. There is no such thing as 'one man, one vote,' and everything is segregated—from schools to restaurants to toilets."

"That's terrible. It's like when my mother grew up in Georgia. She had a friend she played with at home, but when they went to the park they had to use separate bathrooms and water fountains," said Dean.

"That was a long time ago?" Mr. Mutwa asked.

"It was in the sixties—only twenty years ago."

"Yes. But it is worse for Africa today at the end of the

twentieth century. We have a bill of human rights but no freedom and justice, no equality," said the doctor.

"Based on your character and not your color," Johann commented.

"Yes," he responded.

"Think of Martin Luther King," said Harold.

"I know," the doctor said. "We need what Dr. King was fighting for—a Declaration of Human Rights."

"We have one," Dean said.

"Oh really?" the doctor inquired.

"We have a covenant we make each year in the school. On one side are our rights. On the other side are our responsibilities," Nicole said.

"Fascinating," he said.

"We create 'We believe' statements and then 'We agree' statements on how we will behave," she went on.

"It works?" he asked.

"Yes it does," replied Dean, "because everybody is clear and we know what we've agreed on."

"An oasis of peace, this school of yours?" the doctor inquired.

"Well, yes it is," said Nicole. "Kino said that when he came here after Japanese school, this school was like an island."

"It is safe and tolerant and supportive?" the doctor asked again.

"Oh yes," the students agreed.

"In the International City of Peace and Culture," Mr. Mutwa commented. "And I like the way you link rights and responsibilities. We must do that, too." Turning to Nicole, he asked, "And where are you from?"

"From Canada," Nicole replied.

"Oh really," he said, noticing how her ebony skinned glistened in the sun. "And your parents?"

"My father is from Trinidad, and my mother is from Quebec. Her parents are from Kenya," she answered, understanding the question behind his question: You're black. How can you be from Canada? It was like the Japanese who assumed that if she was black she must be from the United States. It made her angry.

Noticing Nicole's frustration, the doctor asked, "So who are you really?"

"Remember that play *Our Town*?" she asked. "I'm Nicole," she said, "a young woman from Canada on Planet Earth in the Milky Way Galaxy."

"Great earthwoman!" exclaimed Johann.

"You know, my children," said the doctor, "that the world is really a small planet in the vast universe, and we are all on this ride together. The fate of all of us on this Spaceship Earth is caught up in the death and destruction that was Hiroshima. But it also leaves us with a message of hope. We can stop this madness or we will perish. That is what is happening in South Africa. Change our ways or die."

So ended summer school.

5

A New Beginning

On September 15 students and teachers returned from their vacations to begin another school year in Hiroshima. Kim and Rand Blackford had spent three months in Columbus, Ohio, where their parents taught American Studies. They were back for their second and final year.

Emily was back from Minnesota. "I spent all summer studying Japanese. In fact I lived in a Japanese village back home."

"In Minnesota?" Kim asked, surprised.

"And I became a global citizen too," she said. "In Minnesota there are twenty villages that are part of the Concordia Language Villages. Each village uses one of ten languages. It started years ago with Norwegian and German, but now there are Russian, Chinese, and French and Spanish villages. And even Finnish, Swedish, Danish, and Japanese."

"That's amazing," Mai remarked.

"What's really amazing is the villages are immersion villages. All of the counselors in the Japanese village speak Japanese and over half are from Japan. Everything is Japanese, from the food to the music to the games and all the stuff we study."

"So you're studying?" Kim asked.

"Well, the high school students can earn a year's worth of language credit in one month. We study about six hours a day. The rest of the time is fun stuff, from crafts to sports."

"So that's how you spent your summer away from Japan. Living in Japan in Minnesota?" Rand said.

"You know you are into something 'henna' when you arrive. You have been sent a passport with your photo and name and stuff in Japanese. Then you go from passport control to customs. There the counselors search your bags and if they find any tapes or magazines or candy or stuff from the 'outside,' they take it and give it back when you leave. Then you go to the money exchange and change your dollars into yen. The store sells only Japanese candies and sweets and T-shirts and crafts. Only the pop is American. I loved it there, and I'm going back."

Josh, originally from Malta, had spent two months in Singapore while his father negotiated a new shipping contract; his company built oil rigs in Hiroshima for use in the North Sea. Raina Fox was new. She was twelve and from Portland, Oregon. Her parents were going to teach for a year at the Hiroshima Center for Conflict Resolution before they moved to Israel. Raina had cerebral palsy. It was a "mild" case, requiring her to wear a leg brace, but "mild" was a misnomer. Raina said "mild" was about as disgusting a label as "handicapped," "disabled," "physically challenged." When you can't run and you want to, and when you spend forty-five minutes every night having your leg massaged, and when people sometimes stare at you or feel so sorry for you—it can be annoying, even maddening at times. Then there is the fear in dreams and down-in-the-mud times when you are worried about whether it will get worse. But Raina was cheerful, had guts, and was a person who would never ever give up.

Andrea Frank, age thirteen, from Holland was also new to Japan and the school. Her mother was Indonesian and a nuclear scientist at the Radiation Effects Research Foundation (RERF) in Nagasaki. Nagasaki was the second and last city to be destroyed by an atomic bomb, three days after Hiroshima. Nagasaki is on the southern island of Kyushu, a one-hour plane ride or a five-hour train trip from Hiroshima. Although it is Japan's most historic international port, there is no international school there. So Andrea, whose Dutch father, Jan, was an internationally acclaimed potter, came to Hiroshima International School every other week for a week's home stay with RERF families. (And people thought Harold's three-hour round trip each day was "so far.") The other week she studied Dutch language and history at home in Nagasaki to be ready to attend high school the next year in Amsterdam. Andrea already spoke English, because she had spent two years at the International School in Jakarta.

And then there was Mr. Morris. He had come from Vancouver, British Columbia, with his family, including Dan and Anna, who joined the middle-level classes. Mr. Morris would teach humanities and social studies to the senior-level classes.

❧ Getting to Know Hiroshima

For weeks after the Peace Ceremony an idea had been germinating within the International School community. Individuals were having thoughts, dreams, and conversations about the ceremony, the interviews, the radio program. Students were talking with each other; teachers were meeting and planning. The experiences had been unsettling for many and had raised questions, concerns, and insights. It was becoming obvious to some that neither teachers nor students, even those who had lived here for years, knew a lot about Hiroshima. And it was clear that some of them wanted to know more about the city's history, culture, and significance. Many wanted to know more about the events surrounding the dropping of the atomic bomb and its aftermath, including its impact on Hiroshima and her people today. What was its significance for the world and for each student and teacher personally? The idea that was forming had not been crystallized into a concise, clear statement, but something was pushing students and teachers to move beyond their current awareness and understanding. A feeling was in the air, and it was growing in the hearts and minds of the people who inhabited this small oasis of international friendship, this island sanctuary in the heart of Hiroshima.

Japan was already at the core of the school: Everybody studied Japanese language and culture at least three times a week, and Japanese arts and crafts, camping, and field trips were an integral part of school life. This was all part of the school's philosophy, particularly of the principal, Mr. Enloe, who had gone to school in Japan at international schools. He felt that his schooling had placed an undue emphasis on language and rote learning and had neglected cultural education. The school's brochure explained that people should leave Japan with an appreciation for Japanese culture, respect for all people, and an understanding that all people share certain human commonalities. Everyone needs not only sustenance and shelter, but also play, laughter, and storytelling. All cultures show appreciation for beauty and skill, and all have needs and aspirations that are expressed meaningfully in diverse ways. Mr. Enloe liked to point out that we could transcend a particular time and place if we could imagine ourselves on the moon, looking at the whole earth. Then we could conceive of our human interconnectedness.

But in the school's emphasis on cultural education, Hiroshima itself had not been a focus. Until now. The need to learn more about the place, its history and development, its peoples' traditions and lives, as well as the legacy left by the Atomic Age, seemed to grow spontaneously among the school community and spread like a field of wild flowers.

Every year the first days of school were spent almost entirely in building school community, an annual rite of passage for old and new alike. The work and play included a "get to know you" party, as well as school meetings at which rules and expectations were discussed and covenants about "what we believe and how we agree to behave with each other" were formulated. There were class assignments of school responsibilities, which included cleaning public spaces (such as hallways) and organizing and running school meetings. New staff and students were welcomed. The calendar for the year was reviewed. There was a school field day followed by the annual "clean the neighborhood park" project, and then a school party, involving everyone from students to office staff and bus drivers, culminating in a picnic of international foods—everything from hot dogs and sushi to seaweed ice cream and vegemite sandwiches.

In one of the senior class discussion groups, the topic of field trips came up. Every year individual classes and the whole school went on overnight field trips to interesting places in western Japan. As they reviewed last year's trips, students thumbed through portfolios of each adventure. These included brochures, maps, sightseeing guides, and photographs from the trips. The school had buses and enough camping equipment for each student to use, whether the trip was to an established camp or involved backpacking to an isolated site.

Mr. Rehlin mentioned that teachers had been discussing the idea of focusing part of the studies on Hiroshima and that some field trips might include a trip or two to significant historical sites in the area. Raina asked, "What do you visit related to the bomb?"

"Do you mean Peace Park?" Mai responded.

"Yes, but also places you read about in books—like Sadako's story," said Raina.

"You mean her home and the hospital or her school?" Kim asked.

"Yes, places like that, I guess," Raina pondered.

"Well, Peace Park is about all I really know," Kim continued. "You know, a hospital and retirement home for atomic bomb victims is right across the street."

"A lot of us spend time hanging out around Peace Park," Mai said. "We know it pretty well."

"Doing what?" Raina asked.

"This summer we got interviewed and we were at the peace ceremony doing a broadcast on radio. And we met a lot of people from all over."

"Cool. Was that fun?" Raina asked.

"Well, it was exhausting," said Mai, "and to tell you the truth, a bit depressing."

"Why?" Kim asked.

"We found out a lot about the buildup of weapons, and

people are still dying from radiation, and it was just too much to think about," Mai said.

"You can't do anything about it anyway," Raina commented.

"This summer in Columbus different groups held peace ceremonies," said Kim. "Rand and I went to a Girl Scout program at our church. They had folded a thousand cranes and knew Sadako's story."

"You're in the Girls Scouts?" Raina asked.

"No, but a friend of my mom's knew we were living in Hiroshima," said Kim, "and so we were sort of on display. It was embarrassing because everybody assumed we knew this and that about the bomb just because we lived here."

"They were fooled!" Mai said.

"So were we," said Kim.

"Well, it was sort of like that here," Mai said. "I mean, these reporters thought we knew a lot about Hiroshima and all the bomb stuff, but we didn't. I know how to fold cranes, but we didn't know anything about all the stuff that happened ages ago."

"But it's right now too, isn't it?" Kim asked.

"I think it's happening now," Raina added.

They were silent for a moment.

❧ Living School

Senior-level meetings continued. These daily and weekly forums to decide issues of school governance were also for solving problems, celebrating, and enjoying performances. Outside of some basic educational matters, the students took responsibility for their lives at school.

Most had seen the class schedule that was posted in the commons. It was not much different from last year's. The teachers liked to group topics together and stretch the limits of individual subjects through interdisciplinary studies and thematic projects. Since students came from at least ten different countries and would leave after one to three years, it was both impossible and unacceptable to teach a standard American or British curriculum. Instead of traditional English or language arts or communications classes, students took "literacy and semiotics" or "inquiry and experimentation." These umbrella topics could include some uncommon areas of study that would stretch both students and teachers. Questions to investigate were large issues: What does it mean to be literate? What does it mean to be symbol users and meaning makers? What are the relationships among spoken language, dreams, and drawing?

This year the schedule was:

8:30	Class meeting (school meeting Wednesdays)
9:00	Logic and maths
10:00	Literacy and semiotics
12:00	Inquiry and experimentation (every other day)
12:00	Physical education and service (every other day)
1:00	Lunch and leisure
1:40	Culture and sociality, term 1: Hiroshima—Past, Present, Future
4:00	Buses leave

Starting in kindergarten, students learned through investigating topics or working on projects that involved both personal and group inquiry. Projects, which took weeks or months to complete, introduced a variety of perspectives and concepts; topics were more short term. Both resulted in individual and class portfolios. Teachers often compared projects to putting on a school play in which the students write the play, build the stage, make the costumes, design the sets, illustrate the posters, act, direct, produce, manage the stage and lighting, sell tickets, and act as ushers, then afterward break down the set, clean up, turn off the lights, and write the review for the school paper.

New students adapted to the circumstances, particularly when they experienced the goodwill and excitement of the community for their school life and studies. Although students didn't have much to say about whether or not they would study, they had much to say about how and what they studied. The program, based largely on student interests, student choices, and authentic ways of learning, was both demanding and stimulating. Students pushed and supported each other through enthusiasm and interest, not competitive grades. Classes were nongraded and crossed age groups, and students had a large say in their report cards, since they were portfolios of their work and included self-evaluations. When students returned to their home countries or moved to other countries, portfolios were good demonstrations of what they had studied and how they had developed. Generally, students enjoyed what they were studying.

But Hiroshima? This was a new topic that raised some questions, especially among the older students.

"I'm interested in studying how to get out of here," Curtis yelped.

"I'm interested in knowing more in case I get interviewed again," Junior said.

"Me too," Raina said, "and I haven't been yet."

"You won't unless you're going to stay another ten years until the fiftieth anniversary of the bomb," Janelle said.

"Don't you think there will be some interest next year?" Isaac inquired.

"Nope," Dean said.

"Only decades count!" Curtis declared.

"Should we call this Wide Island Studies?" Kino asked.

"The building of Hiroshima's bridges and dikes?" put in Dean.

"If we're going to live here, maybe we should know some stuff about the place," Janelle said.

"Well, I've gotten along pretty well so far," Isaac said.

"Not this summer, dude," said Dean.

"Same for you, guy. You speak Japanese in a Hiroshima dialect, but you don't know much either," Isaac replied in Japanese.

"I think it'll be fascinating," Raina said.

"I want to meet the Hiroshima Carp baseball team—especially Kinogawa. He's awesome," said Curtis.

"I want to drive a test car down at Mazda," Junior said.

"I want to go to the Kamikaze museum," Johann added.

"What?" Dean asked.

"I was reading about this the other night. Etajima Island, about twenty minutes out from Ujina Port, was where the Japanese naval college was. It was the headquarters of the imperial fleet—the one that bombed Pearl Harbor. And there is a museum to all the flyers who killed themselves by flying their airplanes like bombs into ships—some 9,000 young men. Before each one flew off, a photograph was taken, along with a lock of hair," Johann explained.

"Kamikaze means divine wind," Mai interjected.

"Most of those flyers were younger than seventeen," Johann added.

"Gross way to die," Mia said.

"Die-hard believers do it today. In Iran, Palestine, and other places people kill themselves for the cause they believe in," Johann added.

"That's a hard way to go," Isaac commented.

"The Japanese fliers thought that by dying for the emperor, who was thought of as a god, they would go to heaven," said Johann.

"Well, I want to be buried in Miyajima Island—the first person to be buried there," said Isaac.

"Sure," Mai said.

"Really—no one can be buried there," Isaac stated.

"We know," she replied.

"Well, we'll bury you in one of the caves next to our campsite—before we kill you, that is," Mai said.

"When are we going?" Junior asked.

"Two weeks," Mai said. "Isaac, Kino, and Dean and I are responsible for organizing it."

❧ Researching

The following week the class voted to devote ten hours a week of class time and five hours a week of homework time for the next several months to get the Hiroshima topic planned, researched, and completed. After much discussion, the class divided up by pulling assignments out of Mr. Morris's old top hat. (The hat sat on a cabinet behind his desk and he also sometimes used it when he imitated famous characters.

There was a rumor that he had been a professional singer and tap dancer, and people were waiting eagerly for the school's annual Culture Festival to find out.) Three colors of cards designated the three tasks of planning the project.

Encouraged by the students' interest, the teachers decided to resurrect the Hiroshima Studies Program that they had originally developed during the 1980–81 school year. The goals of that program had included the following.

1. To enrich participants' life-experiences in Hiroshima, to educate about living in Hiroshima and Japan today, and to develop an understanding of the history and role of Hiroshima as the International City of Peace and Culture.
2. To develop a curriculum that may be used by future students and that may serve as a prototype for similar programs in other countries.
3. To integrate geography, history, social studies, ethics, mathematics and problem solving, science, art, reading, and writing in relation to affective/social experiences to facilitate understanding of these subjects in general and the "Hiroshima story" in particular.
4. To help participants understand conflict resolution and ethical decision making, to facilitate awareness of global issues, and to ensure that participants, when they move back to their home countries, can understanding and speak intelligently about Hiroshima.
5. To facilitate understanding of cooperation among people and awareness of the threat of nuclear proliferation, to encourage children to make wise ethical and political decisions, and to promote tolerance, respect, justice and conflict resolution as the basis of peacefulness and peacemaking.

More concrete objectives of the Hiroshima Studies Program included the following.

1. To develop a basic understanding of the history of Japan using concepts from anthropology and archaeology.
2. To understand the basic historical development of the Hiroshima area.
3. To understand the issues and controversies surrounding the atomic bombings.
4. To understand Hiroshima as the International City of Peace and Culture.
5. To meet and learn from hibakusha mentors.
6. To increase skills in subject areas through integrated topic work on Hiroshima-related projects.
7. To understand physical and emotional and social ramifications of atomic bombing.
8. To understand workings of such organizations as Peace Culture Foundation, World Friendship Center, Atomic Bomb Museum, and RERF.
9. To understand global issues including global nuclear proliferation.
10. To facilitate moral decision making and problem solving.
11. To study the peace movement and work of the United Nations.
12. To develop a sense of empathy regarding bombing experiences through readings, interviews, Hiroshima epicenter walks, folding paper cranes, digging for tiles along river, and so on.

Over the next two weeks one group researched, organized, and led the senior class field trip for the first week of October. It was to be a three-day excursion that included visiting some of the earliest human settlements in the area beginning with Miyoshi, then Hiroshima Castle, and then the majestic Miyajima Island. Students in this group worked with the trip coordinators and with Ms. Yingling and Mr. Yaguchi to plan the trip. They first researched the sites to get cultural and environmental information. They organized the itinerary and financing for the trip, determining campsites, entrance fees, and bus expenses, and they planned meals and snacks and bought supplies. They also aired out and cleaned sleeping bags, air mattresses, tents, and eating and cooking utensils. Afterward they would organize a class presentation and portfolio of the trip.

The second group took on the task of writing several essays on Hiroshima's history up to the present. They also collected materials from their research that would support the other groups' efforts. Their papers used an inquiry approach by asking some original guiding questions and then writing paragraphs answering the questions. The group decided what other materials to present to the class, including facts from travel guides such as *Hiroshima Prefecture* and *Japan Travel* and works of historical fiction such as *Black Rain* and *Hiroshima*.

The third group was charged with the task of communicating with Hiroshima residents, hibakusha, and world leaders on the Hiroshima experience and Hiroshima's significance for the world. This was Curtis's idea. Students wanted to contact people who may have lived or visited Hiroshima in earlier years. Curtis had looked through Mr. Enloe's collection of *Foxfire* books and had read about Elliot Wigginton and his students interviewing local people to preserve the traditional stories and folk culture. After much discussion, the students drew up a list of people to interview locally, as well as prospective correspondents. They ended up writing to the United States' ambassador to Japan, Mike Mansfield, and to Pope John Paul, among others. They also wrote to several peace groups in Europe and the United States, and they wrote to potential interviewees in Hiroshima, including peace activists Rev. Tanimoto and Ms. Shibama, leaders of the World Friendship Center and a hibakusha Volunteer Support organization, officials at the Peace Culture Foundation, the head of the Radiation Effects Research Foundation and, at his request, a parent who was commander of a U.S. military base on the inland sea island of Etajima.

Mrs. Nobori, the school's bookkeeper, and Mr. Yaguchi, head of the bus drivers, agreed to be interviewed. Both were hibakusha. Mrs. Nobori told Mai and Harold that she was happy to be interviewed, but for every two questions they asked her she wanted to ask them one. And Mr. Yaguchi would be happy to share with them the dream he has had almost every night for the past forty years.

❧ Sample Topics

One afternoon the teacher presented the students with an example of what they might find as they researched their topics. It was a handout titled "Going Back in Time" and it utilized the volumes of *Time* magazine in the library's microfilm collection.

> There is no infallible way of telling [Chinese and Japanese people] apart. Even an anthropologist, with calipers and plenty of time to measure heads, noses, shoulders, hips, is sometimes stumped. A few rules of thumb—not always reliable... Japanese—except for wrestlers—are seldom fat; they often dry up and grow lean as they age. The Chinese often put on weight. The Chinese expression is likely to be more placid, kindly, open; the Japanese more positive, dogmatic, arrogant. Japanese walk stiffly erect, hard-heeled. Chinese, more relaxed, have an easy gait, sometimes shuffle.
>
> —*Time*, Dec. 22, 1941, from "How to Tell Your Friends from the Japs"

Questions:

1. What is the historical context?
2. What are the prejudices and stereotypes?

Pearl Buck, who wrote *Dragon Seed* and *The Good Earth*, grew up in China and spent summers in Nagasaki. With Norman Cousins and John Hersey, she helped provide support to Hiroshima after the war. Rev. Tanimoto's children, who started the No More Hiroshimas movement, spent summers at Pearl Buck's home. Here is a letter she wrote to *Time* magazine that was printed in the January 5, 1942, issue.

> *Time* used the words "yellow bastards" and "Hitler's little yellow friends" in speaking of the Japanese. I suggest that none of us use the word "yellow" in speaking of the Japanese, because our Allies, the Chinese, are yellow.
>
> In this war we must, I think, take care not to divide ourselves into color groups. The tide of feeling about color runs

very high over in the Orient. Indians, Chinese, Filipinos, and others are sensitive to the danger point about their relation as colored peoples to white people. Many Americans do not realize this, but it is true, and we must recognize it or we may suffer for it severely. The Japanese are using our well-known race prejudice as one of their chief propaganda arguments against us. Everything must be done to educate Americans not to provide further fuel for such Japanese propaganda.

Questions:

1. What were relations like between "colored" and "white" people in the United States in 1942?
2. What arguments were the Japanese making to other Asians about American morals?

Here is a portion of an essay written for *Time*, August 20, 1945, by James Agee:

> The race had been won, the weapon had been used by those on whom civilization could best hope to depend; but the demonstration of power against living creatures instead of dead matter created a bottomless wound in the living conscience of the race. The rational mind had won the most Promethean of its conquests over nature, and had put into the hands of common man the fire and force of the sun itself.
>
> Was man equal to the challenge? In an instant, without warning, the present had become the unthinkable future. Was there hope in that future, and if so, where did the hope lie?
>
> ...When the bomb split open the universe and revealed

the prospect of the infinitely extraordinary, it also revealed the oldest, simplest, commonest, most neglected and most important of facts: that each man is eternally and above all else responsible for his own soul, and, in the terrible word of the Psalmist, that no man may deliver his brother, nor make agreement unto God for him.

Man's fate has forever been shaped between the hands of reason and spirit, now in collaboration, again in conflict. Now reason and spirit meet on final ground. If either or anything is to survive, they must find a way to create an indissoluble partnership.

Questions:

1. How did the atomic bomb change the world?
2. What do you think about the last paragraph of the essay?

6

The Study Begins

The bus roared through Chugoku Gorge, following the meandering Ota River, past small rice and vegetable farms. Tennesssee's governor, Lamar Alexander, had recently published a coffee-table book called *Friends* that compared Tennessee and Japan through photographs and text. The mountains in southern Japan are similar to the Smokey Mountains, which separate Tennessee and North Carolina. They are wet and misty, with beautiful rounded tops.

The bus came out of the mountains to the Inland Sea, some thirty minutes from Hiroshima. There, about ten minutes away by ferry, lay the majestic and cedar-pine-covered Miyajima Island, one of Japan's "three most scenic" places. It was a sacred island. For thousands of years, religious rules forbade births and deaths on the island. Although the rules were no longer in force, the dead were never buried on Miyajima. Instead, the bodies were sent to the mainland, where they were purified through a series of Shinto spiritual rituals.

The ferry landed next to Isukushima Shrine and the bus disembarked. In the distance, in the middle of the water, was the impressive Torii, a red camphor-wood structure of two trunks, each sixteen meters high and two meters in circumference, and a twenty-three-meter crosspiece, forming an awkward goalpost. It is a symbol known throughout Japan as the entrance into a sacred place of the ancestors' souls and the spirit world. Built in 811 A.D., the shrine is dedicated to the daughter of a Shinto god and is composed of a series of galleries and buildings linked by wooden flooring. It was built over the water in such a way that when the tide is high, the shrine seems to float on the water.

Not far from the entrance is a five-story, 30-meter-high pagoda that was built in 1407 and mixes Chinese and Japanese architectural styles. Next to it is the dark and haunting Buddhist Senjokakuu, or "Hall of 1000 Mats," built in 1587. The group took in these sights as the bus wound its way through small villages hugging the coast to a large beach and campsite the International School used several times a year.

There the group began to settle in. After dinner the students stacked wood in a large pile on the beach. This would become a bonfire after dusk. But first everyone hiked to the cave near the water. Some fifty meters long, three meters wide, and three meters high, the cave had been an air-raid shelter during the war. Walking through to the other side, you come out on a small beach facing Hiroshima Bay. About twenty kilometers in the distance are Hiroshima and the surrounding Inland Sea islands.

Sitting on the beach, Kim and Mai began to collect pieces of colorful dried paper from what was once several lanterns each more than a meter tall and a meter in circumference. Perhaps they had been discarded from a temple or had fallen overboard from a passing fishing boat that had used the light to attract fish to the surface. In either case, they had served their purpose and ended up on this beach. Constructed from tree pulp and bamboo strips, it was beginning to disintegrate, but now the students were giving it a new purpose. As other students frolicked in the water, Kim and Mai began to fashion the paper into messages of peace, folding and folding, making crane after crane. Students who were exploring tide pools, telling ghost stories, and waving flashlights in the cave gradually began to observe the folding and to join in. When they returned to the main beach for the bonfire, they took the lantern with them, and throughout the evening they folded and folded and folded.

❧ First Reports

Several days later, the group whose job was to report on Hiroshima's history delivered their first presentation. It was written by Niraj, Janelle, Junior, and Curtis.

Early Days by the Ota River: A History of Hiroshima

When did people first settle in the Hiroshima area?
What kinds of evidence is there?
Why might they have settled here?
Where did name Hiroshima come from?
Who built Hiroshima Castle?

Hiroshima is located on the Ota River, which flows to the Inland Sea and the Pacific Ocean. This area is abundant in both river and ocean vegetation and animal life, both water and land. In addition, several islands are located in the estuary, where the river meets the sea, providing a safe haven from enemies and wild animals. At the bottom of one of these islands, today known as Hijiyama Hill, a large shell mound from the Jomon period (5000–250 b.c.) was excavated beginning in 1948. Not only shells but fish and animal bones were excavated, and also unearthed were many tools and earthenware (for which the Jomon period is named). Archaeologists speculate that these people traded with other peoples because their tools were made from stones not found in the Hiroshima area.

Other sites found by archaeologists include shell mounds and garbage pits from the Yayoi period (250–100 B.C.) on other islands close to the estuary. It was during this time that people became less hunters and gatherers and began to farm vegetables and especially rice. They lived in small groups or clans and there was a great emphasis on warrior leaders. Each clan had a major manor house or castle. Close to Hiroshima is the great tomb of Saijo (Mitsujo Old Tomb), over 250 feet long and 30 feet high, that was probably for the most important leader of the clan. It was built in the last part of the fifth century. Around this time different areas of Japan were unifying as many clans formed alliances to protect themselves from other groups. This created for hundreds of years a civil war throughout the islands. Whichever alliance of clans had the most powerful armies would control the other groups.

Japan has had the longest ruling imperial family in the history of the world, though they seldom had the power to really rule. They were generally figureheads of a past history in which they were direct descendants of the gods who created the islands and people. Real power was in the hands of the warriors with the biggest armies, strongest alliances, and moist land to grow rice, the staple and money crop. The system was very feudal, with the warriors in control and the priests and artisans having some freedoms, but absolute control was held over most of the people, who were poor peasants. A similar system developed in Europe. Over time the Shogun (the warrior general of the strongest clans' lords) took over leadership, and for several hundred years there were periods of war and then truce between the largest three alliances.

From the eighth century, religion took on a more central role of influence, and hundreds of Buddhist temples and Shinto shrines were established. At Miyajima Island in the tenth century one of Japan's most important religious sites was established. In the middle of the twelfth century, the Taira clan, representing a weak central government in Kyoto, took over western Japan. They made Miyajima's Itsukushima Shrine into a national monument and brought in priests from Kyoto. Over time the Taira clan was defeated in battle by the more prosperous Minimoto group, who established the Kamakura as Shogun or warrior president in 1192 for all of Japan.

This new government chose the Mori clan as chief servants of the central government and sent the clan to the Hiroshima area in 1336. Over time the Moris conquered all the clans in the area. Terumoto Mori, the great-great-grandson of the original leaders, brought many warriors and they established Hiroshima in 1591 by building a large defense structure. Later they were to build a castle and a city, but they too were defeated by other warrior groups until the Asano family took over, representing the Tokugawa government, which ruled all of Japan from 1619 to 1868. Japan was finally unified but closed off to the rest of the world. Thus "shima guni" or island mentality grew even stronger. Hiroshima City was gradually built up by draining the water and filling in with dirt and by building retaining walls on each side of the six tributaries that formed the "wide islands" that became Hiroshima. At the center of the city was the castle surrounded by a large moat.

The history of Hiroshima, its first thousand years, is long and mysterious. Only with such records as shells and artifacts and local myths do we know anything about the area before the sixth century. Then Buddhism came to Japan from China and with it a writing system, so stories and histories could be recorded by the priests. Then local governments were established and people learned to write and keep records.

❧ Organizing the Program

Over the following weeks, the students and teachers organized a study program based on their stated goals and objectives, including field trips, project and research proposals, and readings. Readings were made by personal choice from a variety of history and social studies materials, as well as literature that included John Hersey's *Hiroshima*, Eleanor Coerr's *Sadako and the 1000 Cranes*, Betty Jean Lifton's *A Place Called Hiroshima*, Ibuse's *Black Rain*, the comic book *Barefoot Gen*, and a collection of writings including *Children of the A-Bomb*, in Japanese *Hibakusha*, and in German *Children of the Ashes*. There were also films available from Hiroshima Archives, such as *Hiroshima Mon Amour* and the children's film *Children of the Paper Crane*. Lifton's *Death in Life* was available for mature readers, and there were more technical books such as *Hiroshima and Nagasaki: The Physical, Medical, and Social Effects of the Atomic Bombings*.

Students and teachers had already decorated bulletin boards with borders of Japanese colored papers and had hung cranes from the ceiling. Photographs and papers would join maps and drawings on the walls as the project grew. Calligraphed on a large sheet of rice paper was a poem by noted journalist and children's author Betty Jean Lifton, who had once lived in Hiroshima:

To begin with—
This place you've come to see called Hiroshima
is no one place.
There are many places, each bearing that name.
One is located in the past.
One in the present.
One in the future.
Understand—
The legendary place that you seek
is not located on a map.
It is a state of mind.

About a week after the first report, a second paper was presented. This one was written by Christina, Dean, Raina, Kim, and Nicola, and it joined the class portfolio on Japan. It was based on eight different historical accounts, two of which were in Japanese.

Hiroshima: The Military City, 1873–1945

What does it mean that Hiroshima was a military city?
What role did Hiroshima play in World War II?
How did Hiroshima become a target for the atomic bomb?

In the late nineteenth century, as Japan ended its self-imposed separation from the rest of the world, it also began to reorganize locally and nationally. After a short but difficult war, the government was back into the hands of the emperor and his imperial court. The samurai system and feudalism were abolished and in their place the clans that controlled large areas established, through a central government, state or prefectural governments.

In Hiroshima a railway line was established, linking Hiroshima to Osaka and Tokyo. A large port, Ujina, was built, allowing Hiroshima to be the largest port in the east and south of Japan, close to China, Korea, and Russia. In 1873 the central government created a large army base with the Hiroshima Castle as headquarters, and in 1889 a city government, Hiroshima, one of the first in Japan was proclaimed Japan's first Military City. In 1894 war broke out with China, and the Ujina port became the major staging area for troops and supplies. More people moved to Hiroshima, creating more and more war-related industries, from the manufacture of weapons to uniforms.

Later in 1904, during a war with Russia, the Hiroshima area became even a greater war support area. Close to Hiroshima was

Kure, which became a great warship building port, and Etajima, the island where the naval college was established that became headquarters for the Imperial Navy through World War II. So all around Hiroshima was much industry for warfare. People came from all over Japan to work—so many that when there was a famine in 1885, many emigrated to Hawai'i, California, and South America.

During World War II, Hiroshima Castle was headquarters for the western troops, with some ten thousand troops and some prisoners of war. Large chemical plants and metal industries including Mitsubishi and Toyo Kyogo (Mazda) were built. Young children were moved to the countryside, but thousands of older junior high and high school students were mobilized to work in Hiroshima's war industries. However, until the atomic bombing, Hiroshima was never attacked by American bombers, though Kure and other nearby cities were. Until August 6, 1945. There is some controversy over the dropping of the atomic bomb, though of the seven histories we studied, five argued that the dropping of the bomb was the quickest way to end World War II.

Since the military took over Japan, by 1930 it became a samurai culture again. Children were taught in school how to march and to use guns and bayonets. The Japanese army tried to take over more of the Asian continent as it had done earlier in Korea; it began conquering parts of China. Japan and the United States had been adversaries for years, particularly over Asian resources. The Japanese bombing of Pearl Harbor in 1941 brought the United States into war with Japan but tensions were already there. Some people link directly the bombings of Hiroshima and Nagasaki with Pearl Harbor but many historians saw other factors. One was the Soviet Union declaring war on Japan in late 1945 causing the United States to want to demonstrate its superiority to its risky ally who, as communists, wanted world dominance so the United States dropped the bombs to show its power. But remember the US was the last major power to enter the war as it had been in World War I—very, very reluctant to use force. It took Pearl Harbor to push her over the edge of direct involvement. And who can forget Japan's barbarous killing of large civilian populations in Asia and its inhumane treatment of prisoners of war. Its Samurai mentality and superior view of itself was part of its ultimate defeat, one author noted. Supposedly its Greater Prosperity Sphere was to free Asians from European dominance, but it actually replaced it with Japanese power dominance and the slavery of others.

Another idea was that the Japanese had begun targeting large civilian populations in China and the Philippines, as had the Germans in Europe with the British and Americans following, so it was a given that places like Hiroshima would be bombed. Another historian pointed out that the Japanese were close to defeat and were looking for a way out and probably would have surrendered by October 1945. One history book also noted that President Truman and many Americans hated the Japanese and wanted the quickest end to the war. But another perspective was that the Japanese people were so brainwashed and controlled by the military and Emperor that they would have died house to house and would never give up. The battles on Okinawa showed that the Japanese were very resistant and thousands of civilians killed themselves rather than be taken prisoner. Estimates were up to five hundred thousand American casualties and several million Japanese causalities would result if the Americans invaded the Japanese mainland, and it would take months to end the war. Finally, it was well known that both the Germans and Japanese were trying to develop atomic weapons. Would they have used them on America if they had had them? We believe so for no other reason than the 20th century has had more killing of people than any other century and is just another example of humans' inhumanity to other human beings.

Some things we've learned from all of our studies is that a decision was made by President Truman and his cabinet based upon the advice and counsel he received and his own best judgment. To understand a historical fact—an atomic bomb was dropped on Hiroshima—requires multiple perspectives and points of view. There are many sides to an event, like when five people are at a traffic light and two cars collide. How it happened, who was at fault, who did this, and what about that—these questions require all five witnesses and the people in the cars to talk and see if they can arrive at the "truth." What you discover is many points of view about the same event.

In the end, are killing and war part of our genetic code or part of our learning environment? Can we improve? Has the world become a better place over thousands of years or are we the same? As one peace activist we interviewed said, "In war everybody loses something. There are never any real winners because humanity always loses part of its humanity." This a difficult issue with many perspectives. Who is right? Who is wrong? And who is partly both? Are we born evil or do we learn it?

There is an old saying, "The truth is stranger than fiction." Perhaps it applies in this case too.

❧ A Letter from Norman Cousins

"He wrote us back!" Johann yelled across the commons. "I can't believe it!"

"Who?" Mai asked.

"Norman Cousins, that's who," Johann exclaimed.

"Which one was he?" Junior asked.

"He teaches at UCLA. He's the guy who helped out in Hiroshima by raising money for orphans and the bomb victims," Johann said.

"Well, what does he say?" Emily asked.

"Let me see. Okay. Dear Johann and the Senior Level. What does Hiroshima mean to me after so many years? Go to Peace Park and find next to the Dome the place marked by two rock gateposts that was once a private hospital. You are at the center of the explosion. Stand there in silence and ask yourself, What does Hiroshima signify to me and to the world? For you are at the center of the atomic explosion, the epicenter of the Nuclear Age. I am impressed and deeply moved that you future citizens and leaders are wrestling with such powerful questions. Sincerely, Norman Cousins"

"Wow, that's great. Let's go there," said Junior.

"Wait. We've got to meet with the rest of the class. Look, he also sent this paper." Printed across the top in red ink was NOT FOR DISSEMINATION. In black letters across the center was written "Draft for Power Book" and the title "Visit to Hiroshima 1949." The text later appeared as a chapter in Mr. Cousin's book *Anatomy of Power*, and the author sent an autographed copy to the school's library.

BACK IN CLASS students began sharing the projects they had decided to work on based on their research and communication with various people and organizations. Everyone had chosen two people or organizations to write, telling them of the study project and asking questions such as "What does Hiroshima mean to you?" "Does Hiroshima have a role to play in the peace movement?" "What is Hiroshima and Nagasaki's significance for today's world and our future?" The students completed two additional essays and gave them to the class for discussion and review.

Harold, Heather, and Nicole prepared their paper called, "August 6, 1945: Hiroshima's Ground Zero."

August 6, 1945: Hiroshima's Ground Zero

Early Sunday morning, an aircraft passed over Hiroshima, setting off an air raid siren. People went into shelters but came out after 7:30 and went about their daily lives. At 8:15 the atomic bomb blew up over Hiroshima, creating an atomic explosion and fireball that wiped the city off the face of the earth. It was the equivalent of 15,000 tons of TNT. A huge thermal cloud of fire and smoke rose thousands of feet into the air and made everything on the ground totally dark. Thousands of people died instantly and many more died in the next days and months and years from injuries and radiation poisonings. In the flash of the atomic bombing, the city of Hiroshima vanished. The target of the bomb was Hiroshima Castle, but the bomb missed by 500 meters and exploded directly over a hospital. Thousands of soldiers died. The hospital vanished into dust.

Two days later, Nagasaki was destroyed by the second atomic bomb, and finally several days later the Japanese government surrendered and the war stopped. It took Hiroshima years to rebuild. The Japanese government and American leaders tried to hide the bomb's destruction, especially the thousands of people sick and dying months and years later from radiation-related diseases—diseases of radioactivity which are incurable. There is still debate on how many people were killed, but over 100,000 is a safe figure according to most sources, with another hundred thousand dying from directly related diseases. The government in 1947 established with America and Australia the Atomic Bomb Casualty Commission. This place angered many bomb victims because ABCC did not treat—only studied—people, like "rats in an experiment" and "Guinea pigs." People were not helped by the federal government either, for there was no formal government help until 1953, and finally in 1957, twelve years later, a medical law was passed to help all victims of Hiroshima and Nagasaki.

Two years after the bombing on August 6, 1947, the first Peace Memorial ceremony took place in a park that would later become part of Peace Park. The mayor, Mr. Hamai, read the city's first peace declaration. He said, "These fearful weapons have made the people of the world recognize clearly that a war fought with nuclear weapons would mean the annihilation of human beings and the end of civilization. This must lead us to the realization of unconditional peace and to the birth of a new way of life and a new world." In 1948, Rev. Tanimoto, a Methodist minister, started the No More Hiroshimas movement, which spread around the world, with some people recognizing Hiroshima as a symbol of world peace. In 1949 the central government passed a proclamation making Hiroshima "Peace Memorial City."

Then Hiroshima began building Peace Park and began making plans for a Peace Foundation and Peace Research Center. These were finished in 1955, the year young Sadako Sasaki died at age twelve from the A-bomb disease, like hundreds of other children. But the students in her school, and later other school groups, began raising monies to build a statue or monument for the children. The Children's Monument was built in 1958. In 1962 the American School was established. This later became our International School and the International School of Peace, with our new school attaining accreditation, nonprofit foundation status, and a new building in 1985. From the basement of a church on Peace Boulevard in 1962 to the International School of Hiroshima Prefecture in 1985, the school has come a long way.

Andrea's report came next. She called it "The Short History of Nagasaki: From Wonders to Ruins." As she handed it out to the class, she explained that she decided to do a project on Nagasaki because she was living there this year and because she was part Dutch, Indo-Dutch, in fact. Also she wanted to study this topic because when she heard some of the history of what happened there she wanted to find out more.

The Short History of Nagasaki: From Wonders to Ruins

Nagasaki is the capital of the prefecture of Nagasaki and is located on Kyushu, the large island south of the major island of Japan, Honshu. The limited flatland is surrounded by mountains and faces the South China Sea. During the late nineteenth and early twentieth centuries, Nagasaki's mountains were a vacation spot for foreigners coming from Nagasaki as well as from Shanghai, China. The novelist Pearl Buck, who grew up in China, spent summers in Nagasaki. The farmland is used for rice, sweet potato, and mandarin orange production. Fishing is very important and includes flounder and halibut. For years coal was mined, first for manufacturing iron products and, after Japan opened its doors, for steamships from around the world. The major industry now is ship building by Mitsubishi Heavy Industries. Today the population is about 400,000. In 1949 a national university, Nagasaki University, opened and included the older Nagasaki Medical College. Nagasaki has one of Japan's deepest harbors and is well sheltered by mountains on both sides of the harbor. Nagasaki began as a small village, and when Portuguese traders arrived in the sixteenth century, the government allowed them to come on Japanese land at Hirado in Nagasaki Prefecture, and this is little Nagasaki Village.

The Portuguese introduced guns and Catholicism to Japan. Francis Xavier, a Spanish Jesuit priest, was the first Christian missionary to Japan. He would later become a saint. He came from the Portuguese colony of Goa on the western coast of India to Japan in 1550. Over a short period of time there were many converts to Christianity, including the local warlord or daimyo. Over time, however, the Japanese government became concerned about the thousands of new Christians and were afraid they would lose control of the local people. Because the government was afraid of the religion and its priests, they banned Christianity in 1587. In 1597 six foreign missionaries and twenty Japanese Christian brothers were crucified by the Tokugawa Shogunate in Nagasaki. In 1636 Nagasaki Christians organized a rebellion against the government. Over two years, more than 30,000 Christians were killed. Then in 1639 the Portuguese, along with the Koreans and Chinese, were kicked out of Japan, and except for Nagasaki port, which was open only to Dutch traders, Japan closed itself on the rest of the world for several hundred years. Even the Dutch were not allowed on Japanese soil.

The Japanese built a small island called "Dejima" in Nagasaki Port, which is where only foreigners could live. These "red beards," as the Dutch were known, introduced Western science to Japan and, from what they learned from the Japanese, taught Europeans Japanese medicine (acupuncture and moxibustion). In 1745 the Shogyen allowed Japanese to learn Dutch and read Dutch books, and Dutch residents taught French, English, and later German. Through Dutch-educated people, many Western works were translated into Japanese, including Sir Isaac Newton's physical theories.

Technological advances from the West entered Japan through Nagasaki. Glass blowing began in Nagasaki. Also the first clock built in Japan, the first photography studio, the first iron bridge (and later the first bowling alley) all came to Japan through Nagasaki. Since most of the Dutch scientists in Nagasaki were physicians sent to serve the Dutch residents, major advances were made in medicine. Japan's first school of Western medicine opened in Nagasaki in 1825. Some of these doctors studied the botany, geography, history, language, and culture of Japan and upon their return to Europe published books. At the University of Lyden in the Netherlands, a Museum of

Ethnography was created in 1788 based largely on Japanese artifacts, plants, and animals. This became an important collection for spreading the "Japanese artistic style," which became very fashionable in the late nineteenth century in Europe.

After Japan was opened in 1853 Nagasaki expanded its foreign settlement off the island and on the hills surrounding the port. The foreign settlement was the only place foreigners could live and the place where Japanese could not unless they married a foreigner. It was governed not by Japanese law but by British law. Many countries opened consulates there, including Britain, France, Holland, Russia, and the United States, for business and the transfer of technology. The first steamship built in Japan and the first newspaper began in Nagasaki. One foreigner leader whose home and garden are tourist attractions was a Scotsman, Thomas Glover, who came to Japan in 1859 at age twenty-one and lived the rest of his life in Nagasaki after marrying a Japanese woman. He studied the culture in great depth and made his living selling arms and building ships. He brought the first steam train to Japan and built the first steamship. He founded the shipyards that years later were the primary target for the atomic bombing.

Even though Christianity was banned, hundreds of families continued to practice their faith secretly. In their homes, for example, they had statues of Buddha or shrines to their ancestors, on the back of or inside of which would be images of the cross. They became known as the "hidden Christians." In 1853 Commodore Perry was sent by U.S. President Fillmore to visit Japan with his "Black Ships" (smoke from steamship chimneys). Over the next years, Japan opened its doors to trade and visitors. Soon Nagasaki would become known for its Western influences and its more open attitudes towards foreigners. Besides the shipbuilding and the atomic bombing, Nagasaki is best known today as the setting for the famous opera Madame Butterfly, by Giacomo Puccini, first performed in 1904. It is the story of U.S. Navy officer Captain Puccini and the geisha Cio Cio-san. It's an interesting opera according to my sources, because it takes place only inside a Nagasaki house and it is there that he compares her to a butterfly. It is also a simple plot. Woman wins man. Woman loses man. Woman commits harikiri (ritual suicide). Today Nagasaki is a very beautiful city; its people are friendly; it takes peace seriously on the local level, more even than Hiroshima.

"What are you researching next? RERF?" asked Isaac.

"No. RERF Nagasaki and Hiroshima are the same organization doing the same work: studying the effects of the bomb on people," Andrea replied. "What I want is to find people stories about the lives of these victims."

"What are you thinking of?" Mai asked.

Andrea opened up her notebook and found her notes. "Next I'm going to research this place in Nagasaki City my father found called Nyoko-do. It means something like the 'Love your neighbor like yourself' house. It was the home of a famous peace doctor, and there is a museum next door. That's all I know right now. And our neighbor Mrs. Suzuki says that there are several peace programs in schools. One elementary school has a peace garden with peace sculptures made by kids. I want to find out about that."

"Hiroshima: Yesterday, Today, and Tomorrow" rounded out the first group of papers. It was prepared by Kim, Rand, and Kino and was based on their reading of eight different history books, including two in Japanese.

Hiroshima: Yesterday, Today, and Tomorrow

How has Hiroshima changed since 1945?
What does it mean to be The International City of Peace and Culture?
What do foreigners think of Hiroshima?

Over time Hiroshima became the International City of Peace and Culture and the city flourished, but people continued to die from radiation-related diseases. And as the world got more nuclear weapons and made more powerful weapons, a peace movement was growing around the world. By 1980 the city was designated a major city, one of the "Big Twenty" in Japan, with a population of over 1 million. The American School became the International School, involving families from many countries, and Hiroshima National University grew to over fifteen thousand students, with hundreds of foreign graduate students.

Hiroshima became Japan's major supplier of brushes, needles, tangerines, and oysters. Mitsubishi Heavy Industries builds ships and oil rigs for the world. Mazda Motors expanded and went into partnership with Ford Motor Company. Together they design and engineer small and medium-size automobiles. The Hiroshima Carp baseball team, owned by the public, has won the Japan Series several times in recent memory.

In 1994 Hiroshima will host the Asian games. Many new sports facilities are being built as is a new swimming complex and monorail system. The Atomic Bomb Casualty Commission has become a totally Japanese-run organization, called Radiation Effects Research Foundation. One thing they study is the amount of radiation that is safe for humans to receive from medical examinations and treatment at, say, the dentist's office. Thousands of tourists, from Japan and overseas, come to Hiroshima each year; hundreds of thousands of school students make Hiroshima one of the most famous places for school trips. And each group brings a thousand cranes to place at one or more of the monuments in Peace Park.

Many international visitors have come to Hiroshima over the years. Many have worked hard for peace. Barbara Reynolds started the World Friendship Center. Pearl Buck, Norman Cousins, and John Hersey helped Rev. Tanimoto and others start orphanages and homes for the bomb victims. Our school went to hear the Pope speak in 1981. U.S. Senator Kennedy, Prime Minister Nehru from India, and Secretary General of the United Nations, Mr. Javier Perez de Cuellar all visited Hiroshima and International students got to meet them.

The future for the world is bleak and dark many say because the world is full of weapons and distrust and hatred and war. The United States and the Soviets, along with France, England, and China, have enough weapons to destroy the whole world. The countries of India and Israel may have them too. The Cold War is still very cold. Hiroshima attracts world conferences on peace and friendship and disarmament. The policies, however, of the big countries still seems to be MAD—mutually assured destruction of both sides.

What can we do? Pray a lot and hope the mad people go away? What can students do? We can say we will not be like the adults now in charge. But can we really be different? Should we start Children Crusades like they did back in Europe in 1212 A.D. to take back the holy lands? Can we build peace? Perhaps our view is best shared by Hiroshima poet Toge, who died from A-bomb poisoning in 1953:

Give Back the Human
Give back my father, give back my mother;
Give grandpa back, grandma back;
Give me my sons and daughters back.
Give me back myself.
Give back the human race.
As long as this life lasts, this life,
Give peace back.
That will never end.

❧ Messages from around the World

Over the next two weeks students received letters from the Stockholm Sweden Peace Institute, ambassador to Japan Mike Mansfield, the Fellowship of Reconciliation, and others. Jean-Louis Sainz, Head of Press for the International Peace Research Institute, wrote,

"Yes, Hiroshima has an important role to play in the Peace Movement. It is with Nagasaki the only historical example of people being killed by a nuclear weapon. We must always keep in our minds August 6, 1945, and try to create at an international level peaceful conditions for better understanding between peoples and nations of the world."

Ambassador Mansfield wrote to congratulate the students on their peace studies project and to suggest that *"studying conflicts and resolutions between peoples is the basis for better decisions in the future."* He also suggested that students write U.S. President Reagan. They did.

Helen Caldicott, founder of the highly respected Physicians for Social Responsibility, wrote:

"I do think Hiroshima and Nagasaki have roles to play in the Peace Movement. As the two cities that actually experienced the consequences of nuclear weapons, they can be symbols and speakers for peace. You should work with hibakusha to get the message of the destruction caused by nuclear war out to the world, and do everything you can to try to rid the world of nuclear weapons. This is not only the job of Hiroshima and Nagasaki but of all the world. We need to work together on this, the greatest challenge to face the human race, but these two cities certainly have important roles to play. Thank you again for writing. I'm glad that you are studying this issue, and I hope you will work against nuclear proliferation and for peace."

Bernard Feld, editor of *The Bulletin of Atomic Scientists,* wrote,

"My response to your question 'Do Hiroshima and Nagasaki have roles to play in the Peace Movement?' is I believe Hiroshima and Nagasaki must continue to play central roles in the Peace Movement—their theme must continue to be 'No More Hiroshimas! No More Nagasakis!' The main objective—short- and long-term—of the peace movement is to assure that nuclear weapons will never again be used. To achieve this purpose, the image and lesson of Hiroshima must always be kept vividly before the eyes of the public and our leaders. The danger is forgetting! We must all continue to do what we can to keep this image alive."

Mai received a letter and a small, old book from her grandmother titled *Born Free and Equal* published in 1944 by Ansel Adams. Mai's grandmother was Nisei, or second-generation Japanese American. She lived in Seattle. In early 1942, when she was fifteen, she was one of 110,000 people—men, women, children and even baby orphans—of Japanese descent who were interned in relocation or concentration camps for a number of years. In her letter she wrote,

"Most of them lost their property, businesses and homes. Over 10,000 of us were sent to Manzanar, deep in the California desert, where they lived in a camp surrounded by barbed wire and guard towers. Inside they organized a small American town with community clubs, gardens, baseball teams and Boy and Girl Scout troops. There was a jazz band and even a marching band. From that camp came hundreds of Japanese American volunteers who joined the Army and many of them fought in the most highly decorated unit in World War II. Not one Japanese American was ever accused of espionage for the enemy, though numerous German Americans were arrested. But there were no German American concentration Camps. The tragic secrets of America's past again are uncovered. Mr. Adams, later to be known as one of the world's greatest photographers, spent time there in 1943. Race does matter. And so does being an American. We were hurt most when the babies were brought from several orphanages. The babies looked like the enemy. And so did we, even if we only had as they said, "one drop of Jap blood." Learn from your history darling and never forget your ancestors. Many of them were victims too. I learned much there. I have forgiven but not forgotten the three years I lived there. Love* Obasan Taguchi *grandmother

"What to do with this letter?" Mai wondered. "I will keep it and share it when I find out more."

7

Dean and Isaac's Story

Dean and Isaac made the first presentation to the class based on oral interviews. They had prepared a handout and had several photographs to pass around.

"We went to Nagarekawa Church, over close to Noboricho School, where Sadako went. It's close to the train station," Dean began. "Rev. Tanimoto met us and took us to his office. In that small space he had about as many books as our whole library. Everywhere there was stuff. He was very cool. He has long white hair and is very fit for seventy years old. He asked us lots of questions in English and Japanese, like where we were living and the stuff we do and all about our study project on Hiroshima. He knows Isaac and his family, and he is friends with Isaac's grandparents too."

"He knew about your grandfather too, and he knows your parents," Isaac said to Dean. Then he told the class, "Dean's grandfather was also named Dean, and he is a hero in Japan. He died trying to save many people when a typhoon capsized a ferry many years ago in Hokkaido."

"That's true, but that's another story," Dean said.

"Rev. Tanimoto is a Methodist minister," Isaac continued. "He graduated from Chandler School of Theology at

Emory University in Atlanta, where my father went to graduate school. He had a lot to say, and we wrote up our report based on his interview and all this stuff he gave us—brochures and papers and copies of newspaper articles."

"He also gave us these books," Dean said, passing them out. "They are in Japanese and are copies of speeches and his story, 'Hiroshima and the Atomic Bomb.' And he gave us a biography handout, I guess you would call it, titled, 'A Brief History of the Reverend Tanimoto.' So we mixed it all together in our report."

"We'll read through it and you follow along," Isaac said. "Here are some 3 x 5 cards. Write down any questions you have for us as we go along."

"What stands out about Reverend Tanimoto is that he is bicultural," said Dean. "He studied in the United States. He's Christian. He speaks or reads five languages. He's traveled throughout the world. All his children are bilingual and have studied in the United States. His oldest kids used to spend each summer with the novelist Pearl Buck."

Dean stopped, and Isaac continued, "Because of his A-bomb experience he helped initiate the No More Hiroshimas movement, the Moral Adoption program, the Hiroshima Maidens Project, and the beginning of the Hiroshima Peace Center. The one thing he said to us several times was 'I'm a walking time bomb. I know what I'm dying of. I just don't know when.'"

Then Dean began reading from the biography:

"The Rev. Doctor Kiyoshi Tanimoto was born in 1909 into a devoted Buddhist family. Despite his family's opposition, he became a Christian. On August 6, 1927, he and his parents were on the way to a Buddhist temple when his mother suddenly fell to the ground and unexpectedly passed away. She had been suffering from a slight illness and a heat stroke killed her. At that time Mr. Tanimoto decided to become a minister, and he entered the Methodist university in the Kobe area, Kwansei Gakuin University. His father publicly declared that he no longer had a son and had his family's name erased from the family register.

"Eight years later his father visited him for the first time, unannounced, and asked him to once again be his son. They were reconciled. Several years later Mr. Tanimoto was accepted to Emory University to theology school and graduated in 1940. He then became pastor of Hollywood Independent Church in California, a church for Japanese Americans. In 1941 he returned to Japan, first to Okinawa and then in 1943 to the Nagarekawa Church. Since he was a Christian and had lived in America, he was watched closely by Japanese authorities, though he was not arrested."

Isaac continued,

"I happened to be in the city of Hiroshima at the time of the atomic bomb. It was Sunday, August 6, at 8:15 A.M., that the world's first atomic bomb was dropped. I passed by the central post office, what is supposed to be the center of the explosion, about thirty minutes before the catastrophe, so I could see the city's condition quite well. I went through the city and reached the western edge of it. When I arrived there I saw the flash. And then the noise like a thousand thunder strikes.

"I was behind a hill, standing in the valley in the front of my friend's house. The flash ran suddenly from east to the west. I took a couple of steps into the garden to lie down on the ground between two large rocks, and then there was a strong blast of wind. When I got up, the wooden house behind me was destroyed, and the concrete wall at the entrance was turned over. I saw a few people appearing from under the debris. An old woman appeared before me saying, 'I'm hurt, I'm hurt.' She was bleeding from the head, so I helped her and took her to the first aid station three blocks away. And there I saw many injured people. From there also I could get a panoramic view of where Hiroshima was, and the whole city was on fire and covered in smoke.

"Being anxious about my family and church, I started down the hill into the city. I rushed down the hill. Everywhere everything was destroyed or damaged. I met a long and endless line of people heading up the hillside away from the burning city. Most were injured. They were burned and bleeding. Some had no clothes. Many had burned hair and eyebrows and many had skin from their faces and arms peeling and falling off. I thought it was a procession of ghosts. They didn't cry. They didn't say a word. And they didn't show emotion in their faces, but their eyes were full of fear. Just looking toward the hillside and escape.

"I crossed two bridges into the city, and I saw every house and building was completely smashed to the ground, and then I heard people crying from underneath the debris from here and from there. Everywhere. And smoke and fire covered all the city. I tried to help some, but I couldn't get anyone out. No one could. Everything was on fire. One of my friends came into the central park of the city and found a burned out smouldering streetcar full of human ashes. A body of a man was standing at the entrance, holding the rail to board, putting his foot on the step; this man was merely a burned skeleton. In other words, all the unfortunate passengers on that trolley were burned to ashes in a millisecond."

Isaac stopped and paused. Dean commented, "Then Rev. Tanimoto showed us a piece of roof tile made of clay that had melted into a clump. Scientists say the heat was over 6000° Celsius, hotter than the sun's surface. This tile looked like tiles some of us found last year when we were digging in the river by Peace Park. Rev. Tanimoto said that right after the bombing people began using the phrase 'white bone in a moment.' Thousands of people died instantly and were turned in a moment into white bones. Mr. Tanimoto couldn't get through the city that day to his family or church, so he stayed next to the river. He heard people in the river crying for help, so he took a rowboat and went into the river."

"You all know that Hiroshima means 'wide islands.'" Isaac said. "It divides into six or seven smaller rivers from the large one coming out of the mountains onto the delta and into the sea. Rev. Tanimoto said this next experience happened down on the river where we saw flying kites last spring with students from the Language School Friendship Club."

He continued to read:

"When I got out into the river I heard people crying. There must have been fifteen people, and they were all drowning. I neared with the boat and said to them, 'Get in.' But they were trembling. I took one of them by the arm, but I pulled off his skin. Then I put my arm on this back to pull him up, and I saw he was terribly burned all over his back. I got others in and went to the bank, which was full of people. Everyone was sick. I was almost stepping on them.

"I tried to pass a cup of water from one to another. They were terribly burned and swollen—sometimes twice as large as normal size. No one could be recognized from the other. But with much trouble they raised their bodies to accept a bit of water with their terribly swollen hands. They couldn't bend their fingers. After they drank their water, they pushed away the cup with expressions of thanks, all in silence. I was deeply moved by their courage. They had not given up hope. After many hours of giving people water I was exhausted, and I lay down among the injured and spent the whole night. The next morning I found many of them to be dead, but during the night I never heard a cry. No crying. Only silence. Of course they suffered tremendous pain, but they suffered in silence. They endured quietly together and alone.

"I found the destruction of people terrible, but the more terrible things were not the catastrophe itself but in the hearts of human beings. War is terrible, terrible, terrible."

"Then he asked us about our Hiroshima Study Project, and we told him about it," Dean said. "Then he told us about his projects for the past forty years. First he was interviewed by John Hersey, who wrote about six survivors in a story for *New Yorker* magazine that was eventually published as a book, *Hiroshima*. In 1948 the Methodist Board of Missions invited him come to America and tell his story of Hiroshima and to raise funds to rebuild his completely destroyed church. From 1948 to 1950 Rev. Tanimoto visited 256 cities in 31 states and visited 472 churches, giving over 600 speeches in fifteen months.

"He preached on the need for mission work throughout the world based on his personal story of the Hiroshima catastrophe. Thousands of people had died, but many more miraculously survived. He believed something had to be done for all those injured and, worse, those getting ill from radiation poisoning. Neither the American or Japanese government did anything; only private organizations were providing some assistance. Almost all of Hiroshima's survivors, he believed, wanted lasting peace and no more Hiroshima.

"Many survivors began to embrace the idea of making Hiroshima a Mecca for peace. They dreamed that there might be concrete ways to help world peace: not only medical care and rehabilitation centers but educational programs and a peace research institute. Mr. Tanimoto wrote down his evolving idea as he traveled, but none of the reporters at each place showed any interest. Finally he sent his idea to author Pearl Buck, who showed great sympathy and deep concern for the Hiroshima story. Mr. Tanimoto said when Pearl Buck was growing up in China, she came each summer to Nagasaki. She introduced him by letter to the writer and editor Mr. Norman Cousins, saying 'This is the man who can do something for Hiroshima on a worldwide scale.'

"So Mr. Tanimoto wrote to him and sent him his memorandum on starting a project to help Hiroshima survivors. To his great surprise, Mr. Cousins put the essay in his magazine, *The Saturday Review of Books,* as a guest editorial on March 25, 1949, and wrote, 'The Revered Kiyoshi Tanimoto, author of the following guest editorial, has come to the United States on a speaking tour under the auspices of the Methodist Board of Missions. He is seeking American support for his plan, which the editors enthusiastically endorse and with which they will associate themselves.' A few months later Mr. Cousins visited Hiroshima."

Isaac continued.

"In order to make the idea grow and materialize Rev. Tanimoto and Mr. Cousins asked Mayor Hamai, the Mayor of Hiroshima, to prepare a peace petition. With the signatures of over 100,000 survivors, the petition, addressed to President Truman, said, 'In order that no more Hiroshimas might be realized, we sincerely wish you could take the lead in organizing a worldwide organization through enforcing the United Nations.' All the necessary preparations had been fixed and the date had been set for signing with American authorities, but unfortunately the Korean War started, the peace plan was put on hold for months, and the plan slowly faded.

"Though very disappointed, Mr. Cousins came to Hiroshima, and he wrote an essay in the September issue of *Saturday Review* titled 'Hiroshima: Four Years Later.' The last paragraph told about the more than six hundred Americans who had joined Rev. Tanimoto's Moral Adoption Program, providing clothes, books, and money for orphaned Hiroshima children.

"In 1950 Rev. Tanimoto returned to the United States and this time visited more than two hundred cities in twenty-five states, telling of the Hiroshima peace plan and the Moral Adoption Program. In early 1951 he was the guest chaplain who gave the opening prayer before the U. S. Senate.

"At each place he went, Rev. Tanimoto talked of the Hiroshima maidens. This was a group of some forty women who had been students and were terribly disfigured by burns and keloid scars as a result of the atomic bombing. They met as a support group each week at his church. No one was really interested in hearing about these women. The audiences were silent each time he spoke of them. Everybody wanted to be part of the Moral Adoption program, but few seemed interested in helping these wounded and damaged young women. He couldn't figure out why. Later he learned that in America providing medical care was an individual matter, and it was hard to get public or government support.

"A year later Mr. Cousins brought a medical team to Hiroshima, and they selected twenty-five of these women to go to Mt. Sinai Hospital in New York for surgery. They were placed in homes in the Quaker community, and some required as many as six operations. They were given great support emotionally and physically through the Quaker community. Rev. Tanimoto accompanied them and began another ten-month speaking tour.

"One night he was on the popular TV show with Ralph Edwards, *This Is Your Life*. It featured Rev. Tanimoto, and many people were flown in, without his knowledge, to be on the show—members of his family, friends from his university days at Emory, and the copilot of the Enola Gay, the B-29 bomber that dropped the atomic bomb. Behind a screen, hidden from view, were two Hiroshima Maidens. Viewers were encouraged to contribute to the fund for helping these women, and it was the largest one-night TV fund-raiser that had occurred to that time—more than $60,000 was raised.

"Today the Hiroshima Peace Center and much of the ongoing peace work exists because of Mr. Tanimoto. He has been accused of being both a communist and a U.S. agent, of being self-indulgent and self-righteous, but he never gives up. Today he is retired, and he is still active. On the last day of Rev. Tanimoto's ministry, Dr. James Lowry, President of Emory, gave him a special commendation that was organized by fellow alumnus Mr. Enloe. Today Rev. Tanimoto attends the Prince of Peace Church down the hill from our International School. He is writing his memoirs."

During the presentation, students had passed several 3 x 5 cards to the front of the room. Dean read one of these now: "Who accused him of being a CIA agent?"

Isaac's answered, "After the war there was a growing peace movement in the United States and Japan and different reactions to nuclear weapons. Both on the left and right sides of politics people tried to hurt the other side. Rev. Tanimoto was caught in between. He was used and abused by all sides." Isaac had gathered this from listening to his parents talk about Mr. Tanimoto.

The next question was, "What was his role in building Peace Park?"

Dean said, "He was in the beginning just starting a flame of hope for improving conditions for bomb victims and building his church. When he first spoke in America he came up with the idea of Hiroshima as city of peace, but it really had no backing from Hiroshima leaders or people. Mai, do you have that article by him you showed us the other day?"

Mai passed the article to the front. "*Aftermath* is what Mr. Hersey added to his book many years later when he went back and interviewed the six people he first wrote about."

Dean continued, "Here in *Aftermath* is Mr. Hersey's

piece called 'Hiroshima's Idea,' which was published in 1949 in *Saturday Review*. Mr. Hersey says no one except Mr. Tanimoto and Mr. Cousins knew of this plan. It says:

> The people of Hiroshima, aroused from the daze that followed the atomic bombing of their city on August 6, 1945, know themselves to have been part of a laboratory experiment which proved the longtime thesis of peacemakers. Almost to a man, they have accepted as a compelling responsibility their mission to help in preventing further similar destruction anywhere in the world.... The people of Hiroshima... earnestly desire that out of their experience there may develop some permanent contribution to the cause of world peace. Toward this end, we propose the establishment of a World Peace Center, international and nonsectarian, which will serve as a laboratory of research and planning for peace education throughout the world.

"Why did he leave his church?" someone asked. Neither Dean nor Isaac knew the answer.

"Well," Mr. Morris put in, "Most ministers, when they retire, move on to another congregation to give the new minister some breathing space. The Prince of Peace Church down the road was organized by Isaac's grandparents, who have built three churches and a rehabilitation center over the past thirty years. Since the Tanimotos and Enloes are friends, after the Tanimotos retired they came to Prince of Peace Church. Another thing to note is that Rev. Tanimoto started people thinking about how Hiroshima could be a symbol of peace for the world. Now there is a Peace Research Foundation in the city, a Peace Studies program at Hiroshima University, and many organizations dedicated to the original ideals of a peace center for Hiroshima."

"I've been reading John Hersey's book *Hiroshima,* and Rev. Tanimoto is one of the main characters," Mai said.

"It's a powerful book," Mr. Miller commented.

"I think it's great. It's very sad, and terrible things happen, but the people are so real," Mai added.

"Are we going to read it?" Dean asked.

"I hope so," Isaac said. "I looked at it last week but didn't have time to read it. Much of what Rev. Tanimoto gave us is his notes for being interviewed, so I spent time reading that."

"We'll let the class decided in the next weeks. We've got enough copies for everyone, but I believe the class as a whole needs to decide where we go next," said Mr. Miller.

"What's really neat in the *Aftermath* that will be published soon with the original book," Mai continued, "is that Mr. Hersey interviews the characters again forty years later."

"That would be very interesting to read," Raina said.

"The stories about him being on TV in the United States and with his daughters are fascinating," said Mai.

"Mr. Enloe is friends with his daughter Koko," Mr. Miller commented.

"She's in the book too," said Mai. "She meets one of the pilots of the A-bomb plane, and they study her up at the Atomic Bomb Casualty Commission."

"Cool!" Johann yelled.

"Not cool. Take it from me. It ain't cool," Mai said, frowning.

"Okay, I believe you," Johann lowered his voice.

"We need to read that book," Raina said quietly.

❧ 8

Radiation

The bus meandered up Hijiyama hill in the eastern part of the city, past numerous parks and temples, as it made its way to the summit. From the vantage point of the tallest red cedar tree on the hill, one could enjoy a 360-degree view of Hiroshima. Hundreds of years earlier the wooded hill had been an island, but as the city was built up, the water from the estuary was drained and the area was filled in.

At the summit was a Buddhist graveyard, an observation platform with telescopic viewers for surveying the city and the Inland Sea with its beautiful islands, and the controversial Atomic Bomb Casualty Commission, or ABCC, which had been built immediately after the war and was now called the Radiation Effects Research Foundation, or RERF, and was administered by the Japanese government. Here the victims and survivors of the Hiroshima and Nagasaki bombings were studied, analyzed, and diagnosed but not treated.

In the spring the hill became a sea of pink and people organized *hanomi*, or viewing parties, to enjoy the hundreds of blooming cherry trees dotting the hillside. The International School had such a gathering each March in the picnic area of RERF. Forty years earlier, the scene viewed from the top of Hijiyama Hill would have been a wasteland of charred neighborhoods and gray shells of twisted metal and concrete. There would have been no traffic—only people walking or perhaps riding bikes.

The buildings of RERF were large Quonset huts with semicircular metal roofs, the type of building often seen on military bases. The long, one-story structures housed the administrative offices, examining rooms, and laboratories used for studying atomic casualties and the effects of radiation on the largest exposed population in the world. Here the students were going to meet the chief radiologist, Dr. Rappaport, who was from Australia and had worked at the foundation for more than thirty years.

Everybody had read Raina and Junior and Emily's report on "Radiation and Hiroshima." The students and teachers were ushered into a small auditorium that included a small stage. The backdrop was a white wall that had red lines marking off inches and centimeters. Some of the students were working on questions they wanted to ask, some read the brochure RERF had provided, and some took out the students' report and read it again before Dr. Rappaport arrived.

Radiation and Hiroshima

The heat from the sun, electricity from a nuclear power plant, even the sound of a harp or piano. They all have a common trait: they are the result of radiation. Radiation is the movement of energy from one place to another. Radioactivity and radiation, as well as radio and radiate, come from the Latin word radiare, meaning "to give off rays." Radiation is both useful and destructive to human beings.

There are three kinds of radiation in our known universe. Electromagnetic radiation is called light or radiant energy. Sunlight is one form, and it can pass easily through air and through some materials such as glass. Mechanical radiation requires a material medium. It is sound produced by vibration and can move through gas, liquids, and solids but cannot travel through a vacuum. The third kind is particle radiation, which results from natural decomposition (fission) or particles colliding (fusion).

With high-energy radiation, either high-energy electromagnetic energy or charged-particle radiation strikes the atoms or molecules of some substance, which may change their molecular or atomic structure by causing the loss or gain of electrons. This is called ionizing radiation, because the energy of the radiation creates negatively or positively charge atoms called ions. X rays are a form of ionizing radiation, and they are both useful and dangerous. Doctors must decide whether the cure is worse than the disease, for example, with cancer. Ionizing radiation changes chemical properties, atoms and molecules, and living tissues.

Gamma rays and particle radiation are products of nuclear explosions. Gamma radiation, just one part or photon, is a thousand times more than one part or photon of an X ray. Even the briefest exposure to gamma rays is harmful to human tissue.

Researchers measure the harmfulness of radiation in either rads or rems. A rad measures the amount of iodizing radiation absorbed by living tissues. Humans die when exposed to 800 or more rads [which, by the way, does not hurt cockroaches]. About 450 rads of exposure will kill at least 50 percent of those exposed and some people die with as little as 200 rads of exposure. Exposure to as little as 50 rads will damage long-term living tissue, causing cancers and changing the genetic structure of cells.

A rem is the same amount of biological change in human tissue as one rad of X rays. Most people receive about 0.003 rem of natural radiation each year through cosmic rays and other radiation traveling naturally through the body.

We are part of the universe and we're the only creatures we know of who can create tools to destroy our world. The Hiroshima Peace Reader says, "Radiation sickness, heavy or slight, is incurable. Radioactivity is like a bullet that can cause self-destruction of the human race."

A month after the August 6, 1945, A-bomb blast over Hiroshima, some 120,000 people died and 80,000 were injured out of a population of 320,000. Some died from the bomb blast itself and others from burns or injuries caused by the burning and crashing buildings. But most died from the thermal and light rays and radioactivity. Gamma rays and ionizing radiation were released in tremendous doses, killing through thermal heat burns and massive amounts of radiation.

People within a radius of 4 kilometers, or about 2½ miles, were seriously affected by the radiation. Most of those who received a high dose died within a day to two weeks as radiation destroyed blood, bone marrow, and organs. Those that did survive for days or weeks experienced vomiting, diarrhea, and bleeding from gums and bowels. And then they died. Those with more moderate symptoms had loss of appetite, weakness, hair loss, and bleeding from gums. Today, forty years later, people continue to die weekly from A-bomb-related illnesses, including cancers. The malignant neoplasm diseases, including a variety of blood and bone marrow diseases, included various forms of leukemia that killed many children. Now the remaining children are adults and they continue to get sick and many die.

The room was silent as the students read.

The bomb dropped on Hiroshima by a B-29 bomber was the power equivalent of 15 kilotons of TNT. Each B-29 bomber could carry the weight of 5 metric tons. So you would need 3,000 B-29 bombers to drop bombs to equal the one bomb dropped by the B-29 plane Enola Gay. This bomb turned everything—from bottles and roof tiles to people—into charcoal and dust. Today the nuclear cloud is very powerful. The armies of the world have 20,000 megatons of bombs, or the equivalent of 1.33 million Hiroshima bombs that, if they were exploded, would cover 90 percent of the earth. As people continue to die from radiation and other diseases from nuclear exposure, remember the words on the side of the memorial in Peace Park:

LET ALL SOULS HERE REST IN PEACE;
FOR WE SHALL NOT REPEAT THE EVIL.

❧ Difficult Questions

"Do you have any questions about radiation?" Raina asked.

Silence. Perhaps it was the place—a site for the study of atomic bomb casualties and the effects of radiation; maybe it was the topic; maybe it was the particular time in their lives and studies—that silenced them.

"How many people were not found?" Someone whispered.

"Thousands," Raina answered. More silence.

"How many children died?" Someone else asked quietly.

"Thousands," she replied.

"How many children were injured?" Another classmate asked.

"Thousands more," she whispered.

Silence more powerful than a thousand words.

"Were there any foreigners?" Curtis inquired.

Raina and Junior looked at each and shrugged.

"We don't know," Junior said.

"I do," Johann spoke up. "I read a report in one of the books that there were about ten American prisoners of war from B-29 crews—several at Castle and several at Ujina Port—and I think they all were killed."

Ms. Yingling added, "Let us not forget the others. There were also thousands of Koreans and some Chinese who had been forced to come to Hiroshima as slave labor. Korea and parts of China were Japanese colonies. Even today there is not a monument in Peace Park to these thousands of dead."

"There were also several Russian families living close to the old school. They owned bread and clothing businesses, and one woman was a music teacher." Mr. Enloe said. "There was a story in the paper about them and the brother, now in his fifties, visiting the school when he was here several years ago. Several of his relatives died in the bombing."

"Also there was the priest in John Hersey's book, *Hiroshima*," Mai added. "Remember, I told you about it. I think we all should read that book."

"Good idea to bring to class meeting, Mai," Mr. Enloe said. "You might choose to read that book together."

"Can I see it?" Raina asked.

"It is here in my book bag," Mai said.

"That's right, Mai," Ms. Yingling added. "It was Father Kleinsorge, who was priest at the Catholic Church in Noborimachi. He was from Germany, I believe. But he changed his name to Father Makoto Takakura and did the very difficult thing in Japan; he became a Japanese citizen. It was a well-known story throughout Japan. He died about ten years ago."

"There were also several hundred Japanese-Americans who were killed—first- and second-generation Americans who lived in Hiroshima. These were Japanese families who had been living in Hawai'i or California and had moved back to Japan. We can ask Mrs. Nobori, our bookkeeper, about that. Her family moved back." Mr. Miller said.

"Did Sadako die like them—bleeding and vomiting from the atomic radiation?" Kim wondered aloud.

"Probably," Raina said.

"Maybe," Mia added.

"I'm not sure," Dean said.

"I know she died from leukemia," Kim said.

"What does it say in the book? You read that book on her didn't you?" Mai asked.

"It doesn't really say anything about that," said Kim.

"Let's ask Dr. Rappaport when he comes. He would know probably." Junior said.

"I don't know," Raina said, more to herself than to the group. "I don't know."

❧ Atomic Bomb Casualty Commission

Dr. Rappaport was a tall, large man with beautiful silver hair and a large mustache. He wore a white lab coat with pockets full of pens and had a stethoscope around his neck. He looked like a medical doctor. He was a researcher. He spoke energetically, and his hands gestured and moved as he talked. Dr. Rappaport welcomed everyone to the RERF and said how happy he was to hear that we were studying Hiroshima from early times to the present and that that approach would put the work of RERF in perspective.

"You know," he said, "my family was in the original group that started your school. We tried to start the school up here at what was then the ABCC in 1961, but we could not find two teachers we needed, so we began the American School in 1962 down in the basement of the Baptist Church on Peace Boulevard, next to the American Culture Center. Over the next few years, the Culture Center closed, the Baptist Church moved, and the school moved to Ushita, where your present 'old school' is. In the early 1970s it became the International School, in part because Hiroshima proclaimed itself the International City of Peace and Culture.

"Now," he continued, "I want to tell you something of the history of ABCC and RERF and what kind of work we do, and then after your questions I'll give you a tour of our facilities. The Atomic Bomb Casualty Commission was started in 1949 and was sponsored by the governments of the United States and Japan. The United States National Institutes of Health sent researchers and pathologists and biological statisticians to work with Japanese researchers and doctors to study the effects of radiation on the population of Hiroshima.

"This commission was organized during the occupation of Japan by U.S. Armed Forces, which lasted through 1952 and put closure on World War II. We are often asked what role this organization plays in Hiroshima. Why isn't it a hospital? Why are you not treating people? Hibakusha ask that question often. And other people have, too: citizens, government people, peace leaders, you perhaps. Well, that is a powerfully good question and you must frame it in the context of what happened right after World War II in Japan and the United States and in the world.

"There no easy answers, and especially when governments are involved, decisions that are seen as correct at one point in history—at the time they are made and executed—may be questioned or considered wrong later on. I have lived with this ambiguity about Hiroshima and our world and the bomb for the past forty years. I ask that you understand that there are some basic questions you need to consider—or perhaps that you are already considering—in your quest to understand Hiroshima and the Atomic Age:

"1. How was the decision made to drop the atomic bombs on Hiroshima and Nagasaki? 2. How did the United States and Japan respond to the victims of Hiroshima and Nagasaki? For example, why did it take twelve years from the time of the bombing for the Japanese government to enact the A-Bomb Victims Medical Law? 3. What has the world learned from the A-bomb physically or medically, psychologically, and socially? 4. What does Hiroshima mean to you as a symbol of the world's future?

"We recently completed a conference here with scientists from around the world on 'Reassessment of Atomic Bomb Radiation Dosimetry,' in which we looked at our assessment of radiation and recalculated our findings from the past forty years. The most important work we do is to provide medical examinations for Hiroshima residents, both bomb victims and nonvictims. Each year we provide services for thousands of people in the largest and longest continuous health survey in the world.

"Our research is based on where people were at the

moment of the bombing and where they live now, measured in radiuses of 500-meter increments from the epicenter of the bombing.

"RERF is 2,500 meters, or five circles, out from the bombing. These concentric circles are circles of study of Hiroshima citizens' life spans.

"This research assists us in helping doctors and researchers prescribe treatment for patients, and it also tells us the effects of radiation over time. Of course we hope that a nuclear war never happens, but there may be accidents, for example with the radiation leakage from a nuclear power plant or spilled radiation waste resulting from a train wreck, and so on. Our research also gives us information on radiation dosage levels, for example, the dosages you get from radiation treatments for cancer as well as the dosages levels at the dentist's office.

"What we have here is a huge epidemiological and statistical analysis of very large population samples in Hiroshima and Nagasaki. No matter how terrible and tragic the bombing here was, we have much to learn for the future of our planet and humanity. The most important reason for continuing our work at RERF is that no one knows for sure how long radiation remains in humans. The damage it does to these brave people must be carefully studied as long as possible—for them and for us and for your future children's children."

Dr. Rappaport stepped down off the small stage and approached the group. "Okay, any questions?"

There were plenty of questions and concerns and issues and fears and even more feelings that were not articulated.

"How was ABCC started exactly?" one student asked.

"Right after the war, scientists visited this place and saw how dangerous atomic bombs really were. The secretary of defense wrote a report for President Truman and said that Hiroshima would be a unique opportunity to study the medical and biological effects of radiation. In 1947 the ABCC was established, and it has been funded over the years largely by the National Institutes of Health and the U.S. Atomic Energy Commission."

"And how about the first studies of people?" Christina asked.

"From 1948, 2,500 children ages 5, 6, 8, and 10–19 who had been exposed to radiation were periodically examined and compared to 2,500 children named the 'control children.' This led to studying not only the effects on children but hereditary effects, by studying mothers and babies. Beginning in 1950 more than 75,000 people were examined."

"And..." someone prompted.

"We've learned so much about radiation and its dangers, as well as the benefits, the safe level of dosage, say, for the dentist's office and so on," he said.

"What are those lines on the wall up there on the stage?" Mai asked, though she was sure she knew the answer.

"They are for measuring a person's height," said Dr. Rappaport. "Is that it for now? Okay, let's begin our tour. Follow me."

The students got up to follow the doctor out the door. Mai and Kim stayed behind for a moment. "I thought so," Mai said to herself, and she turned to John Hersey's "Aftermath," written years after *Hiroshima* and added to the original version. She found the paragraph on Koko Tanimoto and began to read.

"Koko, the daughter who as an infant had experienced the bombing, had been taken almost every year to the American-run ABCC for a physical checkup. On the whole, her health had been all right, although like many hibakusha who had been babies at the time of the bombing, her growth was definitely stunted. Now, an adolescent in junior high school, she went again. As usual, she undressed in a cubicle and put on a white hospital gown. When she had finished going through a battery of tests, this time she was taken into a brightly lit room where there was a low stage, backed by a wall marked with a measurement grid. She was stood against the wall, with lights in her eyes so glaring she see could not see beyond them; she could hear Japanese and American voices. One of the former told her to take off the gown. She obeyed, and stood there for what seemed an eternity, with tears streaming down her face."

Tears streamed down Mai's face too.

"What's the matter?" Kim asked.

Mai said nothing. She passed the book over to her and pointed to the stage. Kim began reading. She turned to Mai in disbelief and shook her head.

"We've got to do something," Mai said.

"What do you mean?" Kim asked.

"I don't know. Just do something about it," said Mai.

"What?" Emily asked.

"The bomb, we've got to do something about the bomb and...I don't know. Let's get out of here," Mai said.

"Pray to God it doesn't happen again," Emily whispered solemnly.

"It can and it probably will," Kim said in frustration.

"We can do something," commented Mai.

"Kids don't start wars," Kim said," but what can we really do for peace?"

Sadly they went off to join the group as it toured the depressingly gray waiting room, the examination rooms, and the laboratories of death before heading down Hijiyama Hill through the city and back to their school on the mountainside.

9

Peace Walk through the City of Death

Kim was excited. She had just received a letter and a package from the Vatican in Rome containing information for her report on Pope John Paul II's visit to Hiroshima in 1981. International School students had gone to hear him speak, and of the group who went with Mrs. Enloe to hear his address, only Mai remained at the school. Many of the students had met Cardinal Carsoli, Secretary of State of the Vatican, from whom Kim had received the letter. In part it read,

"I do remember well meeting you and your classmates. We also want to thank your school for encouraging other schools in Japan to join in the effort to erect a monument in Peace Park commemorating His Holiness's visit to Hiroshima on February 25,1981, the day I met with you and we talked about peacemaking in the world. The monument reads these words, which speaks directly to your questions on peacemaking and the significance of Hiroshima for the world:

War is the work of man
War is destruction of human life.
War is death.
To remember the past is to
commit oneself to the future.
To remember Hiroshima is to
abhor nuclear war.
To remember Hiroshima is to
commit oneself to peace.

Enclosed you will also find copies of the Pope John Paul's Address on Technology, Society, and Peace. Sincerely Yours in Peace."

To begin their presentation to the class, Mai and Kim read Cardinal Carsoli's letter and then described the pope's visit before handing out "Pope Paul John the Second's 'To Remember Hiroshima.'"

On Wednesday, February 25, 1981, Pope Paul John II came to Hiroshima. He first gave a speech beginning with greetings in nine languages—English, Japanese, Russian, Chinese, German, Italian, French, Portuguese, and Polish—and then spoke about the topic that to remember Hiroshima is to abhor nuclear war and commit oneself to peace. The intermediate and senior levels went to hear him in Peace Park, and later that morning senior-level students met with Cardinal Carsoli. In the afternoon Mrs. Enloe took some students, including Mai, to hear his address on "Technology, Society, and Peace." It was cosponsored by the City of Hiroshima and the United Nations University.

"Ladies and gentlemen, we have gathered here today at Hiroshima; and I would like you to know that I am deeply convinced that we have been given a historic occasion for reflecting together on the responsibility of science and technology at this period, marked as it is by so much hope and so many anxieties. At Hiroshima, the facts speak for themselves in a way that is dramatic, unforgettable, and unique. In the face of an unforgettable tragedy, which touches us all as human beings, how can we fail to express our brotherhood and our deep sympathy at the frightful wound inflicted on the cities of Japan that bear the names of Hiroshima and Nagasaki?

"That wound affected the whole of the human family. Hiroshima and Nagasaki: few events in history have had such an effect on man's conscience. The representatives of the world of science were not the ones least affected by the moral crisis caused throughout the world by the explosion of the first atomic bomb. The human mind had in fact made a terrible discovery. We realized with horror that nuclear energy would henceforth be available as a weapon of devastation; then we learned that this terrible weapon had in fact been used, for the first time, for military purposes. And then there arose the question that will never leave us again: Will this weapon, perfected and multiplied beyond measure, be used tomorrow? If so, would it not probably destroy the human family, its members, and all the achievements of civilization?"

The pope's powerful plea for peacemaking and the ethical uses of sciences and technology that followed this introduction should be place in the historical context of 1981. The Cold War was in full swing between the two most powerful nations, with nuclear weapons capable of turning the planet into ashes of death and black rain. For months the Reagan administration and the Soviet Union, led by Soviet Foreign Minister Andrei Gromyko, had been deliberating about starting meaningful negotiations on a whole range of topics. But the United States' position was that since the

Soviet Union had more nuclear weapons than the U.S., successful negotiations could not begin until the United States "caught up." Only with bigger and better weapons could the United States show the Soviet Union that it was prepared to fight at least a limited nuclear war and that the United States was willing to have up to 25,000,000 civilian deaths. It was thought that only that kind of resolve would convince the Soviets not to push the nuclear button first.

In October 1981 the feature story of ***Newsweek International*** was "The Nuclear Arms Race." The cover showed both countries racing to increase their nuclear capability. The article concluded by raising this critical issue: "The rush to match the Russian nuclear arsenal has confronted Americans once again with a debate in which no civilized person can be entirely comfortable: over the enormous military, economic, and moral issues surrounding nuclear war." A second article in the same magazine was "Thinking the Unthinkable." It said, "As the superpowers talk of a 'winnable' nuclear war, the world becomes a more dangerous place."

Over the years the strategies of the two countries seems to have moved from MAD (mutually assured destruction) to a winnable war. But we two classmates ask you, with talk of a winner, aren't the chances of war occurring even more frightening? The ***Bulletin of the Atomic Scientists*** believes so. That is what they said in a letter we got from them. The building up of nuclear weapons is like a doomsday clock. Or like the clock in Cinderella that was heading toward midnight, when her stagecoach would turn into a pumpkin. If 11 P.M. is a time of perfect peace and 12 o'clock is doomsday, or the destruction of the world by nuclear war, we're now at about four minutes until midnight.

The point is this. Together the United States and the Soviet Union have almost 20,000 warheads, each capable of 80 times the firepower of Hiroshima. The last article in the magazine, "Scenario for a Limited War," gave information on today's bombs' power. Think of the concentric circles that described the Hiroshima bombing. Now, instead of the area within half a kilometer being instantly incinerated, the same destruction would reach out 3½ kilometers. Within 11 kilometers the blast would toss an adult in the air and send debris flying at 100 mph. Within 13 kilometers people would have second-degree burns, and up to 590 kilometers away people would be partially blinded from a single glimpse of the fireball as it rose 12 kilometers into the sky. The ashes of death and black rain, or radioactive fallout, would bring death to millions over the next days and weeks and months and years. Multiply that by 18,000 and you have nuclear winter for thousands of years. So this is Pope John Paul's message:

> In the past, it was possible to destroy a village, a town, a region, even a country. Now, it is the whole planet that has come under threat. This fact should finally compel everyone to face a basic moral consideration: From now on, it is only through a conscious choice and through a deliberative policy that humanity can survive. The moral and political choice that faces us is that of putting all the resources of mind, science, and culture at the service of peace and of the building up of a new society, a society that will succeed in eliminating the causes of fratricidal wars by generously pursuing the total progress of each individual and of all humanity. Of course, individuals and societies are always exposed to the passions of greed and hate; but, as far as within us lies, let us try effectively to correct the social situations and structures that cause injustice and conflict. We shall build peace by building a more humane world. In the light of

this hope, the scientific, cultural, and university world has an eminent part to play. Peace is one of the loftiest achievements of culture. And for this reason it deserves all our intellectual and spiritual energy.

From Hiroshima, Pope John Paul went to Nagasaki to deliver a similar message and to participate in a Mass for the ordination of new priests.

❧ Mrs. Nobori's Story

Mrs. Nobori, the school's beloved bookkeeper, was as diminutive as she was robust. A very fit woman at age sixty-three, she walked three miles every day except during the occasional typhoon or snowstorm. She was a second-generation Japanese American who moved from Hawai'i to Hiroshima at age nineteen, following her husband back to Japan. He was drafted into the Japanese army and died on an island in the Pacific during World War II. She never remarried after the war.

Because of her great acuity in English and mathematics, she got a job at ABCC in 1950. She had recently retired from that job, but she had worked part-time for the past five years keeping financial records for the school. Today she was to accompany the senior-level class to Ushita in the northeast part of the city where the old school was located, across from the neighborhood park.

The park, which was no more than sixty by forty meters, was the only public facility in the area and served the many nearby families and their children. A small one-room building for public meetings stood at one end of the park, and at the other were swings and sandboxes. The dirt ground in the middle was a playing field for kickball and softball. Since parents and small children used the park in the mornings, the International School students came in the afternoon.

Students piled out of the bus with their knapsacks and water bottles. A few had cameras, and Curtis carried a carved walking stick from New Zealand. They headed for the small building, which sat near a large, gray granite monument surrounded by a small fence. Japanese characters were etched on the stone. Mr. Miller gathered the students around the gate.

"Today," he said, "we take the walk we have been planning for so long, through Hiroshima to Peace Park. Thanks to Mia and Dean and Junior for walking out the planned trip last weekend. It took them four hours from start to finish.

"We begin here at this special place. This is where our school was for many years, and when Hiroshima became the International City of Peace and Culture, we became the International School. This is a special place in other ways, too. We are so happy to have Mrs. Nobori with us today. She lives close by this park and was here on August 6, 1945."

Turning to our bookkeeper, Mr. Miller said, "Mrs. Nobori, thank you so much for coming. We're glad you're with us. I hope we can keep up with you."

"You know," he told the students, "Mrs. Nobori walks many kilometers every day—as much as from here to the new school."

"Thank you, everyone, for inviting me," said Mrs. Nobori. "Several weeks ago Heather, Nicole, Christina, and Kim had lunch with me, and they told me about your study project. I am very glad you are studying this topic because it also means much to me, you see, because I am hibakusha too. I was here at this place many years ago—before any of you were born. I have very ambivalent feelings. You see, not only am I hibakusha but I am both American and Japanese. My parents were Japanese immigrants to Hawai'i, and I came to Japan with my husband in 1940."

Everyone was quiet and attentive.

"On the morning of August 6, I was in my home, about five hundred meters from here. There was no sound really. No great flash. Just the rumbling of our house and the terrible shaking and the feel of a great heat wave. The rush of the heat wind was so strong it blew down most of the houses, which were all made of wood as far as you could see. Then we could see the huge clouds of black and the smoke and fires. It just happened in a second.

"Then people started coming out of the wreckage and out of the city. We were all dazed. Many people were injured. Everybody was numbed, and I think all of us were frightened. We didn't know what had happened. We couldn't tell if there were bombs or if an ammunition plant had exploded. But other than the rise of that heat wind, there was no initial sound of explosion. So we didn't know what to think at first.

"But then many people saw the 'pikka don,' in English 'lightning thunder flash.' There was this powerful sound of 'do...dooo...ju...inn...gwann!!!!' A thousand thunderclaps simultaneously. And then there rose this huge cloud of smoke and later came the black rain. Then people started coming toward here. But the people were so many, and so many were bleeding from cuts or burns. Some had their clothes torn off and others wore tattered rags. Can you picture it?"

The whole group now surrounded her and seemed to nod in unison. She looked at and beyond the group. And everyone turned, following her finger as it pointed toward downtown.

"There!" she exclaimed, seeing the strange scene again in

her mind's eye. "From there came the thunderbolt, the pikka don." As she pointed, the students saw a resplendent city built on the ashes and rubble of that not-so-distant past.

"So a lot of people were leaving the city and heading for the hills or the river toward the new school. Many of them stopped here. Some were too injured to continue. Some were old or very young. There was water here from the faucets. And trees—though all the leaves were blown off. And you could see the fireball in the distance. The heat of a million suns. The fires had not reached this spot, though the heat wave had. But the houses around here were still standing. And so here on this ground many people injured from the A-bomb stayed, and many did not leave this place forever. Several thousand people died here on that day and in the days to follow. And they were cremated at this site. Their ashes were left here, and this monument is a testament to them."

It was very quiet. The sun had not yet taken the chill off the morning air. No one said anything, but their hearts and minds were churning with feelings. For here at this sacred place on the ground they were standing on, on the ground where hundreds of the world's children played games, this ground they kicked up and tumbled in, this ground they would make mudpies of—here they played in the ashes of the dead. And until now they never knew it.

Heather opened her bag and took out a garland of brightly colored cranes. She opened the gate and placed them on the monument. Rand took a photograph of the group standing at the monument.

Mr. Miller asked for a minute of silence for reflection and in memory of those who had died there. Some prayed. A few had tears. All were silent.

❧ Peace Walk

"Picture this place in front of you and try to imagine that day years ago," said Mrs. Nobori. "Hiroshima was a desert. There are deserts of ice and deserts of sands and deserts of stone and deserts of water. And there was this atomic desert, desert of death." She stopped and closed her eyes. "Remember this place." Then she stood quietly and the breeze carried her words toward the city.

Then she said, "We are now ready for our journey."

As the group walked, Johann made some simple but surprisingly accurate calculations. Isaac had drawn concentric circles on maps of Hiroshima showing 500-meter intervals starting from the epicenter at Shima Hospital, and Junior and Raina had made maps of Peace Park. Using these, Johann calculated that the school was 3,500 meters from the center of the atomic explosion. Every five hundred meters, Johann would read off how far they were from the epicenter.

As the group walked through the neighborhoods, Mrs. Nobori pointed out places of personal and historical interest. Shadows of people from years ago seemed to hover nearby. Mrs. Nobori pointed out her house and the general area where the fires had stopped. She explained that fire lanes had been constructed throughout the city by tearing down fifty-meter-wide stretches of homes. Then, if there were fires because of bombings, the flames would not jump over the barren areas. These fire lanes were constructed largely by demolition crews of junior high and high school students. Other students worked in factories making weapons, clothing, and field kits.

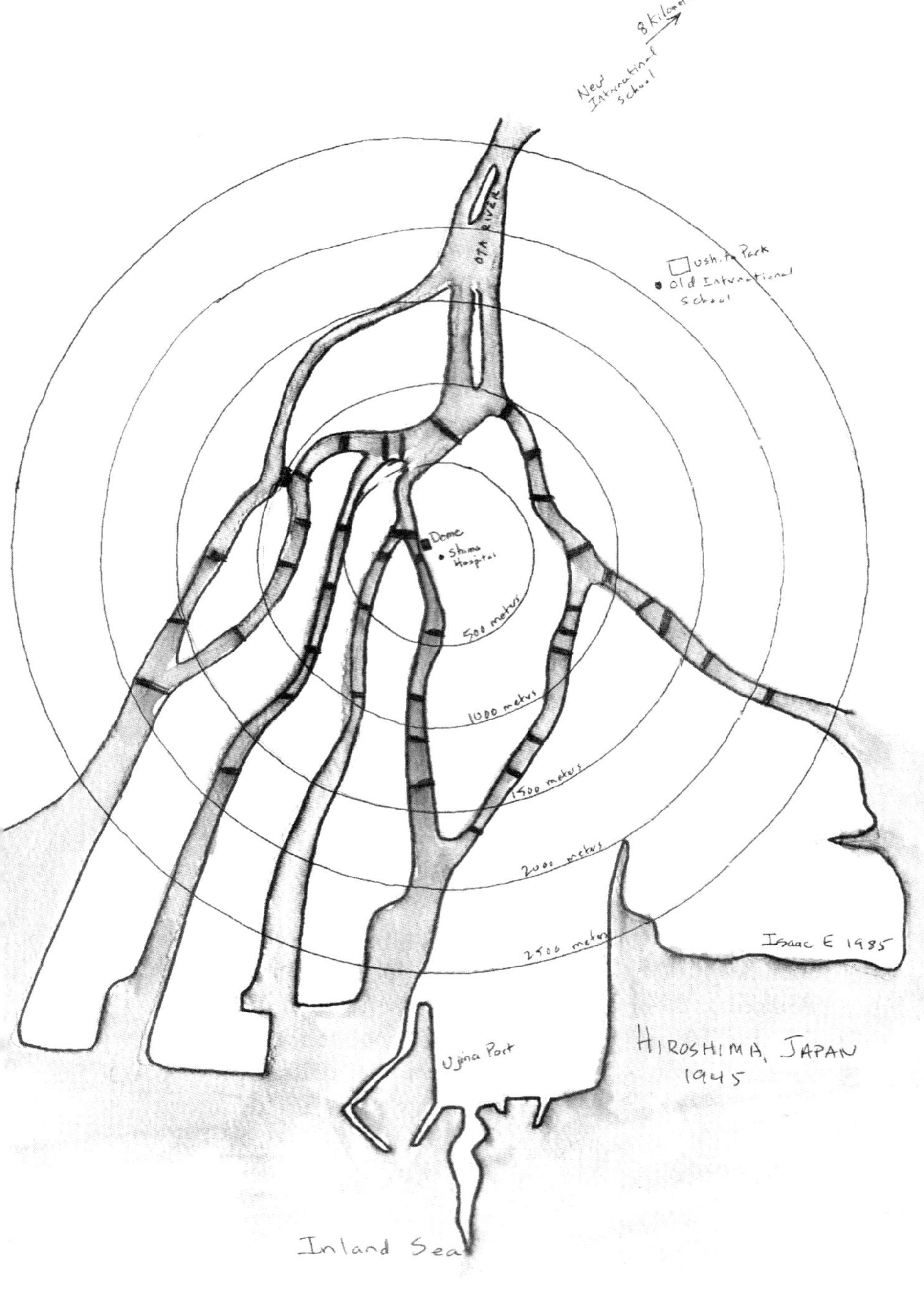

8 kilometers
New International School
OTA RIVER
Ushita Park
Old International School
Dome
Shima Hospital
500 meters
1000 meters
1500 meters
2000 meters
2500 meters
Isaac E 1985
Ujina Port
HIROSHIMA, JAPAN
1945
Inland Sea

Miraculously, Hiroshima's oldest Buddhist temple, built of huge cedar logs, though damaged was not destroyed. After passing the temple, the students crossed the river into the central city. They walked to Shukkein gardens, which were hundreds of years old and famous throughout Japan. The scenic pond and miniature islands created a sense of the expansive Inland Sea with its hundreds of mountainous, pine-covered islands. Here students sat in the shade of the tea house and took out their journals for writing. Mrs. Nobori provided two prompts.

"Please write as you feel," she said. "What is your wish for world peace? And what can you do personally to build peace in your world?"

From where they sat, the students could see small granite markers, about a meter high, on which were mounted copper plates. The plates contained photographs of the vista from the monument after the atomic bombing. The burned and twisted trees and upended bridges formed an alien landscape whose natural features appeared grotesquely familiar but seemed to be of another world. Now in this beautiful garden, in bright sunlight and in the shadows of a beautiful tea house, the students wrote secretly of their thoughts and feelings.

Soon they left the garden and walked several hundred meters to the entrance of Nobori Junior High School, where Sadako and her classmates had gone to school. According to Johann the group was now 2,000 meters from the epicenter of the bombing. The original school had been consumed by fire. In front of the new school was the bronze statue of a girl. Mai read its inscription: "To the children of Hiroshima and the world. Let us work for peace." Heather opened her bag and pulled out strands of a thousand cranes created from recycled papers, including gum wrappers, just as Sadako and Chizuko had done thirty years earlier.

"These are beautiful, Heather," Mr. Miller said.

"Thank you. We have five thousand or so. The last night on our field trip to Miyajima Island we finished them. We started more than a month ago with our friends at Friendship Night down at the World Friendship Center."

"See, the smallest ones are gum wrappers," Mrs. Nobori exclaimed. "And look, this strand is made from Peace cigarette packets."

"Yuck," Raina remarked. "That's disgusting."

"It is ironic," Mr. Miller noted, "that one of Japan's most famous cigarette brands is Peace."

"Was it started before or after the war?" Junior asked.

"Good question," Mr. Miller said.

"It would be ironic if it was after the war," Heather said. "Wishing for peace by killing yourself smoking!"

"Weirdness is everywhere," Curtis added.

"Recycle," Mai said. "Remember Sadako made her cranes from used gum wrappers and cigarette packs."

"The secret of the paper cranes," Ms. Yingling explained, "was that paper was made from nature to send prayers to the gods. The papers with prayers were put into trees surrounding a shrine and then over the years, they turned back into dust of the earth."

"Cycles," Mai said.

"Right," Johann said. "Earth to culture to spirit to earth."

❧ From the Castle to Peace Park

The Castle was the next destination after the school. Everyone proceeded down the wide boulevard past several hospitals, the YMCA, and the city jail toward the east entrance of the Castle grounds. Crossing the moat, they passed the monstrous outer walls of the Castle grounds. Here they were at the original target of the atomic bombing. This had been headquarters of the 2nd Japanese Army. Since the early 1940s Japan had been divided into two military-industrial districts, and Hiroshima was headquarters for western and southern Japan. With more than ten thousand Imperial Army troops stationed here, the Castle was a natural target of the Allies.

Walking through the grounds, the students saw thousands of shards—broken roof tiles from the original Castle roof and its secondary buildings. The new Castle, like downtown Hiroshima, had been rebuilt upon the rubble of the destroyed city. The blast from the epicenter, a thousand meters away, had rearranged the Castle and the moat's walls like a child playing with wooden blocks. The new Hiroshima had arisen like a phoenix from the nuclear ashes of the city of wide islands.

Now the International School students stood on the grassy knoll in front of a large Shinto shrine, the shrine where twenty-year-olds came each year from around the region to pray and be blessed as new adults. The students ate snacks, wrote in their journals, and drew pictures to accompany their writing. After a short rest they began their journey to the area spanning five hundred meters to ground zero. They walked past a beautifully constructed circular building, the Hiroshima City Museum, which was filled with art treasures from around the world donated to the people of Hiroshima as gifts of peace.

Finally they came to the main boulevard through the business district of downtown Hiroshima. Heading west, they reached the Aioi bridge. To their right was the municipal stadium, home of the professional baseball team, Hiroshima Carp, and to their left lay the Atomic Dome and the environs of Peace Park. The dome was the ruins of the Hiroshima Prefectural Commercial Exhibit Hall, which was built, according to Isaac's research, in 1915. The products of Hiroshima were on permanent display and were sold there. The structure was also used for fairs and art exhibitions. (Hiroshima is known throughout Japan for such products as tangerines, needles of all sizes, writing or calligraphy brushes, and oysters. It is also known throughout the world for its Mazda automobiles and trucks and Mitsubishi ships and oil rigs.)

The Exhibit Hall had been located almost directly under the center of the bomb. It was the only building shell, with its metal dome, left standing. And it was the only building the Hiroshima government had left as a memorial and reminder of the atomic bombing. Mr. Enloe commented that when he lived here twenty years ago you could walk up to it, though you were in danger of being hit by falling debris. Today the walls are reinforced and it is surrounded by an iron fence. That is because the mayor, Mr. Hamai, had gone to Osaka and Tokyo and stood on the street to raise money to preserve the dome and had caused a great sensation in Japan. People from all over donated to the mayor's fund to preserve the memorial.

As the students walked past the dome, Mrs. Nobori led them to a gray tower that was about five stories high and covered with ceramic plates. On top, she pointed out, were the Goddess of Peace and eight doves. And on each side of the tower were two plaques, each about six feet high. These showed young people at work and play. One plaque showed girls sewing, and another pictured lanterns floating down the river—this was an annual ceremony in which the candles in the lanterns represented people who had died that year. There was also a plaque showing people working in a factory and another showing students farming.

"More than six thousand junior high and high school students died that day," Mrs. Nobori commented. "Most young children had been moved to the countryside to live with relatives or in special homes away from their parents. But in 1944 the government passed a student mobilization law, which sent all high school boys into the army and all students in middle school or above to work in military industries. This monument represents students from more than 350 schools throughout Japan who were sent without their families to work in the factories." She paused.

"Two of my cousins died here." She closed her eyes for a moment. "About 8,000 students were working that morning. For six months before the bombing, thousands worked each day, creating fire prevention roads that kept the fires started by air raid bombs from spreading. So thousands of students were outside or working in the factories close to the railway station about 1,500 meters from here. Most of those who died were girls. And most of them died instantly."

Standing at the Epicenter

The students moved on to the spot where Shima Hospital had been. Following Mr. Cousins's advice, they stood in front of the two granite entrance posts that were blistered and melted from the nuclear heat and blast. Johann had brought Mr. Cousins's letter and the chapter he had sent. For hours, Johann had practiced presenting selections from the chapter. With the students gathered around the posts, Johann began to read aloud:

I stood at the spot which was believed to mark the center of the atomic explosion. Directly in front of me were two fairly thick and round stucco columns or gateposts on a very small plot raised about one foot off the ground level as a marker and memorial. These columns were all that was left of a hospital, directly under the atomic burst. A new hospital had been built right in back of the old gateposts. It was a two-story affair, painted white. Patients waved to us from the windows.

Johann paused and turned toward the rebuilt hospital, looking from the same spot from which Mr. Cousins had looked. Everyone turned. No one was at the windows this time. Johann continued in a somber voice.

As I stood at the center of the atomic explosion, it was difficult to describe the things I felt. Here, only a few years earlier, there was a flash of heat, which at the split second of fission was many times the surface temperature of the sun. And suddenly, even before a stopwatch could register it, the heart of the city was laid open with a hot knife. I talked to dozens of people who were in it—dozens who were crippled and burned and suffering from diseases of radioactivity—

and the story was very much the same. The sudden flash of light brighter than the morning sun, much more intense than lightening, much more intense than any light ever seen before on this earth.

Again Johann paused. The wind swirled off the river and pushed the heat around the students' faces. They could hear the street noise, but it didn't hold their attention. They gazed across the hospital grounds and ran their hands along the scarred granite posts that still stood as Mr. Cousins had written. Johann continued:

If you lived through that second, you found your clothes were on fire, and you rushed out into the street and ran, for everyone was running—no one knew where. And everything was now blazing and you were inside the fire, trying to run somewhere. Then someone yelled, "Run for the river!" and you threw yourself into the river and thousands of others did the same and you wondered what happened to your family, your children or your parents. No one knew where anyone was, but there were people all around you, and other people were jumping from bridges into the river, and dead bodies were all around you in the river, but you could hardly hear the people crying out because the blaze was like rolling thunder sweeping over you.

Everyone turned and followed Johann's eyes toward the river behind them. Silence. He continued, his voice shaking slightly.

And all day and night the fire ate your city and burned your dead, and all night you stayed in the river to cool your burns, but the tide ran out, and you buried yourself as deeply in the mud as you could and prayed for the tide to come back in again with the water from the sea to cool your fevered body, even though it was salt water and threw knives into your burns, but at least they were cool knives.

For some reason, Johann thought to himself, it was supposed to be easy to read this. He had practiced long and hard, and his mother and father had listened to him, not once but twice. But now it was becoming hard to read in a steady voice. He wasn't giving up, but he was straining to finish; his legs quivered a bit and his hands shook slightly.

The hours passed slowly and you searched the sky for the light of morning, but the city was a torch and it was difficult to see the sky. But then the morning came and you joined the thousands of others stumbling over the wreckage of the buildings, the sounds of they dying and the damned all around you. You were too much in a hurry to notice you had no clothes; it was hard to see that the others had no clothes either, for their bodies were like charcoal.

Johann couldn't finish. His eyes moistened and he was visibly shaking now. He handed the pages to Mai. They hugged. She continued to read the message from Mr. Cousins.

This then was Hiroshima in the first hours of the Atomic Age. It was something new in the solar system— getting at the heart of the matter and ripping it apart, causing the smallest units of nature to smash each other and set off a flash as though a piece of the sun itself had broken away, and sending out strange rays that went through the bones and did things to the composition of human blood that had not been done before or dreamt of before. This was the triumph of mind over matter in the ultimate and most frightening sense.

As I stood in front of the large stone columns from the old hospital gateposts and reached over and felt the rough, raised surface of the stone, its composition altered because it had been melted by the explosion, I wondered why people would ever come back to the city again—not merely Hiroshima but any city—any city that man ever built, for by this bomb he had place a curse on every city everywhere.

All had been touched. Some looked away. Others held tightly closed fists. Some hugged each other. Some closed their eyes. All could feel the warm breeze as it picked up force. A charged whirlwind had been conjured up. A blast of emotion. A shock wave rippled their reflections in the water.

So there they were, these children from around the world who presently called Hiroshima their home. How did they belong? To whom were they responsible? Who was responsible for the place called Hiroshima, this hallowed ground of both death and life at the beginning of the Nuclear Age. Physically numbed, they seemed to be experiencing a kind of emotional fallout.

"Why do you think he sent us this?" Emily asked.

"To scare us?" Raina wondered.

"What did we ask of him?" Mai said.

"Why is Hiroshima so significant to you?" Kim responded.

"How do you feel about what happened in Hiroshima?" Dean added.

"I can't go on," said Mai quietly.

"Me either," Isaac said.

"What's the matter?" Emily inquired.

"I just don't feel good," replied Mai.

Then Mr. Morris spoke up. "Those who want to, go to the children's monument. Two minutes from here. Others can wait here by the river."

The group split up. Mai and Kim and Isaac and Emily stayed. The others went on.

"We'll be back in ten minutes or so," Mr. Morris said.

❧ A Monument to the World's Children

The children's monument was very simple and yet so beautiful. There must have been a million cranes surrounding it. All of the banners and signs accompanying the cranes were in Japanese. Raina had researched the building of the monument. She read from her notebook:

"On the 25th of October 1955, ten years after the bombing, a junior high student named Sadako Sasaki, who attended Nobirimachi Junior High School, died of the A-bomb disease at the Hiroshima Red Cross Hospital, which had been the setting several years earlier for the famous French film *Hiroshima Mon Amour*.

"Until the end of her life she was hoping to recover from her blood cancer disease, and she followed the popular belief that folding a thousand cranes will bring good luck. The outbreak of her a-bomb disease was sudden—she had not been sick earlier and was the junior high 100-meter running champion—and was a great shock to her classmates. They realized even more the horrors of the atomic bomb even years after 1945. Her classmates decided to raise money to build a monument in memory of Sadako and other students who had died or would die and as a fervent desire for peace.

"The idea was developed by the students with the helping hands of some adults, including the school janitor, Mr. Kawamoto, and the idea spread throughout Japan and even overseas. The sponsor was Hiroshima Children and Student Association for the Creation of Peace. More than 3,100 schools in Japan and nine foreign countries contributed.

"The statue is nine meters high. On top is a bronze statue of a girl with her arms stretched high, holding a golden crane. Two statues on each side symbolize a boy and a girl wishing for peace. A bell hangs inside the tower and on it and all over the ground cranes are placed. On the front of the bell is inscribed 'A Thousand Paper Cranes,' and on the back is 'Peace on the Earth and in the Heavens.' Directly under the monument are the words written by a middle school student: 'This is our cry. This is our prayer. To create peace in the world.'

"Cranes come every day from all over Japan, usually brought by students on their field trips. The monument area is cleaned weekly by student members of the Paper Crane Club, still led today by Mr. Kawamoto."

Heather took out the final garlands of cranes and the students laid them out on the monument. Raina straightened the silk banner upon which was written in Japanese and in English: In Peace. The Students of Hiroshima International School.

10

Life and Death Questions

Mai, Kim, Emily, and Isaac sat quietly by the river. A breeze had picked up and it was cool. The tide was out, and from the river wall where they sat, some eight feet from the riverbed, the estuary spread out like a great expanse of brown, deserted valley with a small silver river running through it.

"Let's go down and look," Mai said.

"For what?" asked Kim.

"For relics of the atomic bombing," replied Isaac.

"Is it okay?" Kim asked.

"Sure. We did it last year," Mai told her.

"Is it safe?" Kim wondered.

"You've got to watch out for mudmonsters!" said Isaac.

"Crayfish," Mai interpreted for Kim.

"How about glass?" asked Kim.

"I don't think it's a problem," said Isaac. "Last year we came here with the YMCA. We dug up old tiles from the bombing. They were used to make a wall that decorates the entrance to the Y."

"Over there on the main street?" Kim asked.

"Yes. All of those tiles came from kids who came here last year," Mai replied.

"Why?" Isaac wondered aloud.

"Because they wanted to commemorate the bombing in some way—so people wouldn't forget," said Mai.

"That's interesting," Kim commented. "Remember Mrs. Shibama telling Raina and me that she was afraid when all the hibakusha were dead?"

"What?" asked Isaac.

"That people would forget what happened here."

"How could they?" said Mai.

"Well, maybe not people in Hiroshima, but everywhere else," Kim explained.

"I doubt it," said Isaac.

"I don't," said Kim. "People's memories are very short."

"I'm not forgetting," stated Mai.

"Neither am I," said Kim, "but we live here."

"So?" queried Mai.

"So, we can't get it out of our minds," said Kim.

Their feet squished through the mud and they were quiet for a few moments. Then Isaac commented, "You know something? I've actually had nightmares about Hiroshima since the summer."

"Well, I'm going to after today," said Mai.

"So am I," Kim added.

Using sticks they had picked up along the way, the three of them began to dig in the mud. At first they found only a coffee can, some plastic packaging, and a few shells of contemporary life. For a culture so well known for its appreciation of natural beauty, it was odd that people tended to trash beaches and hiking trails. Then Kim hit something else. Together she and Isaac dug out a large fragment of a house tile. Kim carried it to the stream that meandered through the center of the riverbed and washed it off. One side was common gray tile. But on the other side, the clay had blistered and bubbled in hues of red and brown. Here was a piece of the nuclear age, an artifact from that fateful day. Several more minutes of digging revealed additional tiles.

Mai began humming and then sang quietly, making up her song as she cupped her hands and reached into the water, letting it flow naturally back into the stream, "Water, water, the river of life, flowing back into the sea."

As she sang, Isaac commented, "I was down here last summer. On August 6. On the banks over there by that bridge, people were lighting candles and placing them inside paper lanterns. Then they floated them on the water."

"I've seen that before," Mai said. "The lantern carries a spirit."

"I thought it was just a symbol," Isaac replied.

"Well it is and is not. It is the spirit for each person who died in the bombing. That's why they send thousands and thousands, all lit up and floating toward the sea through the city," Kim said.

"It's a person's soul," Mai said. "We Buddhists believe that your soul stays in the place where it died for forty-nine years before it travels on."

"The lanterns look like fireflies as they get farther and farther away," Isaac said.

"Do you believe in eternal life?" Mai asked. They all nodded.

"But I don't want to die," Emily said.

"We all have to someday," Mai replied.

"But not now!" Emily said.

"Sadako didn't have a choice," Isaac said and then turned toward the bridge where the lanterns with the souls departed each year. "Life ain't fair."

"Let's talk about other stuff," Emily said.

"Life and death. Is there anything else really important compared to that? It covers everything," Mai responded.

"You know that question Mr. Morris raised last week? I've been thinking about it almost every day," Isaac said.

"The forest one?" Mai asked.

"Yes. If a tree falls in the woods and no one is there, does it make a sound?" he said.

"No people? Do the snails and earthworms count?" Mai wondered.

"That's a good question," Isaac said.

❧ Meeting Mr. Hersey

They continued to dig.

"You won't believe who I met this weekend," Isaac said to the others after they had washed the mud from their tiles and set them on top of the riverbed wall.

"Vegetable or fruit?" joked Mai.

"No, seriously," he said.

"The emperor of Japan," said Kim.

"Come on..."Mai said.

"My mom says laughing makes you live longer," Emily remarked.

"Then you'll be immortal," Kim replied.

"We could be playing this game all day," Mai laughed.

"Who did you meet then?"

"John Hersey," said Isaac.

The girls perked up. "You did?"

"We went to Rev. Tanimoto's for lunch on Saturday, and Mr. Hersey was there," explained Isaac.

"Well, what was he like?" asked Kim.

"Nice old man, tall, with gray hair. Distinguished. I told him you liked his book," Isaac said to Mai.

"What did he say?" she asked.

"He asked me if I had read it. I said not yet but the whole class was going to. I told him you had read the new part that was in the magazine."

"And what else?" Mai wanted to know.

"We got to see *This Is Your Life* from 1955—the most popular TV show at the time in America," said Isaac. "On each show they would feature a person and bring on guests to tell about that person's life. Mr. Hersey and Mr. Cousins arranged for the broadcast that featured Rev. Tanimoto."

"What was that like?" asked Kim.

"Well, we'll all get to see it. He had a copy of the tape for my dad."

"Well, come on, tell us about it," Mai prodded.

"The tape is in black and white, and the whole program is set around selling Hazel lipstick and nail polish—the commercials are part of the show and there were models trying to break their nails and putting on glossy lipstick."

"What about the show itself?" asked Kim.

"Well, it's interesting. Rev. Tanimoto isn't gray haired, but it's him. The announcer says, 'This is your life. And who are you?' Then he says, 'I'm Kiyoshi Tanimoto.' And they showed photographs of the atomic explosion accompanied by drumming that was so loud we had to turn down the volume. They told about August 6, and then they had some guests from Emory University and some of Mr. Tanimoto's old friends from Methodist churches. Then you could hear the voice of a man saying something like, 'And looking down on Hiroshima all I could think of was, My God, what have we done?'

"Then this man came out and stood next to Mr. Tanimoto, and the host said, 'Rev. Tanimoto was on the ground and Captain Lewis was in the air and at almost the same moment, at 8:15 on August 6, 1945, you both said, My God!'

"Wow, heavy duty!" commented Mai.

Isaac commented, "Yeah. Rev. Tanimoto said to us, 'I was shocked. I had no idea he would be there and no idea what to say or how to respond.' Next the family came out. They had been flown by American armed forces aircraft from Iwakuni base to Los Angeles—secretly. Rev. Tanimoto didn't know they would be there. Then the host said something like, 'Ten years ago the atomic bombing occurred, but there are many reminders of its great power. Meet two of the Hiroshima Maidens. They are badly disfigured and we do not want to embarrass them, so we will not show their faces.' All you see is a silhouette of the two women."

"Strange," said Kim.

"Who was embarrassed anyhow?" asked Mai.

"My dad said that Rev. Tanimoto remembers how scared Koko was, because Captain Lewis had been drinking and he stood backstage squeezing Koko's hand. She was terrified."

"Anything else?" asked Kim.

"We'll have to see it all together. There's more, but those

are the most important things I remember," said Isaac. "On the way home my dad told me that the Tanimoto family was a bit peeved with Mr. Hersey."

"Why?" asked Mai.

"Well, he wrote some stuff in the new part of the story that you read in the magazine."

"The Aftermath?" asked Mai. "That was written forty years after his original story about Hiroshima."

"Well, he told stuff he shouldn't have," said Isaac.

"Like what?" Emily asked.

"About one of the daughters being adopted," Isaac said.

"So?" Emily responded.

"So it means that she might have difficulty getting married, because being adopted is sort of like being hibakusha," explained Isaac.

"Like Yuri says about reading *Black Rain*," said Mai. "The people were covered with black rain after the bombing and that made them untouchable. The woman in the story can't get married because she is considered to be tainted, and no one other than hibakusha want to marry hibakusha."

"So you see the connection?" said Isaac.

"Yes. I even found out that in Japan when someone is going to get married, the family hires a marriage detective to check on the other person's background," said Mai.

"Come on!" exclaimed Isaac.

"I'm serious," said Mai. "Ms. Yingling told us that she had five different marriage proposals, and her parents had each man checked out to see who his ancestors were."

"My dad said Mr. Tanimoto's daughter Koko also has a tape of the TV show the family was on," said Isaac, getting back to his story.

"That's in *The Aftermath* too," said Mai. "Maybe we can borrow it."

"So we can't get it out of our minds," Isaac said.

"One thing I can't get out of my mind is that Junior and Johann told me earlier that they were going to find the secret room with the boxes of ashes and bones," Kim stopped.

"What are you talking about?" Mai said.

"Johann said Raina's dad told her that behind that grassy mound by the bell—look, over that way," she pointed across the river bank to the park. "That mound with the incense burners in front of it and all the thousands of cranes along the gate is a mound of ashes of thousands of people, and behind it, inside a small room, they keep ashes of ten thousand people they could not identify, in little boxes."

"Terrible," Emily said.

"It makes me sick," Mai said.

"Spooky," Isaac added.

"I wouldn't go inside. You don't mess around with spirits," Kim said.

"Or dishonor the dead," Mai said.

❧ 11

Searching for Truth

Mr. Morris handed out three essays to the students, saying, "Isn't it wonderful to see your adult mentors and teachers contributing to our project?"

"Just like you always say, Mr. Morris. Practice what you preach," Kino said.

"And just like you do every day, Mr. Morris. During silent reading, you read too. You could be correcting papers, but you read with us," Raina added.

"Good point!" Mr. Morris smiled. "Enjoy these essays. One is about the debate last month over our school mascot. Remember our discussion about Richland, Washington, where the bomb was partly developed? The high school there that uses a mushroom cloud as its symbol and calls the basketball team 'the bombers' was thinking about changing its name and mascot. I liked the idea proposed by Mr. Yaguchi, our groundskeeper and bus driver, who was a bomb victim. He suggested we call ourselves 'the doves' and have our emblem be a mushroom cloud covered with birds of peace.

"The second essay is about Mr. Kawamoto, who we will be meeting at Peace Park next week. The last one is by Dr. Enloe's friend Larry Johnson, a teacher in Minneapolis, who with his wife, Elaine, won the first International Video Festival prize in Tokyo this year for a video letter exchange project they started between schools.

"Two of these articles appeared in *Hiroshima Signpost: The English Language Monthly*, written and published by foreign residents in Hiroshima and published by the International School. Walter Enloe wrote the first one, and Swiss educator Gauthier Loffler wrote the second, one of many articles he wrote on his personal journey of peacemaking. Go ahead and spread out through the commons. We'll have our usual uninterrupted silent reading time as you read two of these articles.

"Let me know what you think of the articles by taking good notes on those that provoke you, give you ideas, or raise concerns," said Mr. Morris.

"Interesting points of view," Kim commented.

"Different, very different," Emily added, "And yet they have common ideas to them."

❧ Teacher Stories

The students stopped reading and began to exchange books and articles as they had been doing the past couple of weeks, since Mai had suggested that they read John Hersey's book *Hiroshima*. They could choose which books and articles to read, as long they read more than one.

The class had multiple copies of John Hersey's *Hiroshima*, which originally appeared in the *New Yorker* in 1946, and Mai now had a hardback copy of the book. Johann had brought in *Strahlen aus der Asche*, which was published in Germany and contained the story of Sadako Sasaki and the founding of the Unity Club, the Association for Peace, and the Paper Crane Club. Though the book was also available in English, Johann and Christina were reading the German version. Kim was reading Ibuse's *Black Rain*, and the school had one copy of Betty Jean Lifton's photographic book *A Place Called Hiroshima*, as well as a copy of her husband's book *Death in Life: The Survivors of Hiroshima.*

Other books that were available included a collection of accounts called *Children of the A-Bomb*, stories of survivors called *Hibakusha* (in Japanese), and *Barefoot Gen: A Cartoon Story of Hiroshima*, which had been a well-known series in a weekly children's cartoon magazine that followed Gen through the bombing and its terrible aftermath. Several days ago Dean announced that his parents had discovered a book on Sadako titled *Orizuru no kodomotachi* (Children of the Paper Crane). His parents were going to try to get permission to translate the book into English. Dean pointed out a sentence in the book that said, "By now she [Sadako] had made another 500 cranes, which added up to a total of around 1,500."

"But how about Eleanor Coerr's book *Sadako and the 1000 Paper Cranes*? She said Sadako folded only 644 and died and her classmates finished," Nicole said.

"Maybe Eleanor didn't speak Japanese," said Mai.

"Maybe she read it somewhere else," Dean suggested.

"Good story," Christina added.

"Maybe she just made it up," said Junior.

"Well," Dean remarked, "My dad said Sadako's family was interviewed for the book."

"Maybe we should talk to them too," Isaac proposed.

"They live in Kyushu now," Mai put in.

"Maybe we could write them or telephone them," said Kim.

"Good idea," Emily responded.

"Maybe we should write our own book," Kim added.

"What are you thinking of?" asked Raina.

"Well, we are here and we've been studying this subject," explained Kim. "We have people like Kino and Mai and Isaac and Dean who speak Japanese. We could find out the true story and write it down."

"What is true? Who decides the truth?" Mai asked.

"Maybe one author wants to make a certain point to the reader," Isaac ventured.

"Or for effect," Kim added. "The writer knows little kids would not see Sadako as a hero if she folded a thousand cranes and didn't get well."

"Well she is a hero and she folded more than a thousand cranes and she didn't get well!" proclaimed Emily.

"But we're older too. Maybe we can see more sides to it than ten-year-olds can," Isaac added. "Last night my dad and I were talking and I told him what we were discussing, so he gave me this letter. Look at this letter. It might help us think through our questions." Isaac produced a letter written by his dad's friend Larry Johnson, who had written one of the articles passed out earlier. Larry and his wife, Elaine, were teachers and storytellers.

"Let's read this first and then talk," suggested Mr. Morris.

Sadako: A Story with Many Stories

Every year since 1982, at our August 6 Hiroshima-Nagasaki Remembrance, we have told the story of Sadako, the young Japanese girl who died of leukemia ten years after the bomb was dropped on her city of Hiroshima. The story, compiled from accounts by Sadako's family and friends, as well as various written accounts of the time, is both sad and inspiring.

Today the story is known to many people in the United States as "Sadako and the 1000 Paper Cranes" because of the popularity of the version written by Eleanor Coerr in 1978. When Elaine and I began telling the story, we didn't know of Ms. Coerr's book. Based on the accounts available to us, we wrote our story and have told it at many schools and events throughout the United States and other countries. The storytelling is enhanced by our folding a paper crane and then holding it aloft at the end.

The first time we told the story was in 1982 at a workshop called "Storytelling, TV, and Healing." For us it was a new story that we were ready to try out publicly. When we finished, a woman in the audience stood and said, "That's my story you've told so beautifully."

Afterward, we waded into the audience to meet Eleanor Coerr, who had published a written version of the story, which we promised to look up and promote when we told our story. The meeting seemed fortuitous, but as the weekend progressed, we learned that other attendees believed we had done an awful thing—stolen this woman's story and not given her credit. Of course, the story is really Sadako's, not ours or Eleanor's, and we hadn't stolen it. Nevertheless, we felt ashamed. We wanted to have a conversation with Eleanor Coerr and make sure everything was all right, but how?

We wrote several letters to Ms. Coerr's publisher that were not answered, then we found her name and home address on a list of educators with whom we had contact, and we wrote to her again. We explained how we had heard the story and said that now we always mention her book so that people would know it is available. Eleanor wrote back and said, "Your work is impressive, and I'm glad you continue to use the Sadako story in your repertoire."

We thought that was the end of it, but the issue resurfaced at the 1980s Congress of Storytelling in St. Louis. There was a long ethics discussions that included the question of who owns or doesn't own what story and why. At the reception I was talking with a storyteller from California, and in the course of the conversation I told her about what had happened several years earlier. She gasped and said, "That was you? Out there we still talk about the man who stole this woman's story."

I was hurt and puzzled and didn't know what to say. The notion that a story can be stolen is sad, but we live in a culture that turns things into products that can be marketed, and of course sometimes the notion is valid. But Sadako's is simply a story that needs to be told. "This is my cry. This is my prayer. To establish peace in the world."

"Wow, what a story!" Kim exclaimed.

"Whose story is the story?" Isaac asked.

"Who decides what is truth and the real story?" Mai wondered.

"It seems to me this is a question worth pursuing," Mr. Morris said. And, indeed, the students would find themselves thinking about it a great deal over the next days and weeks. "One thing I know for sure is that Larry and Elaine will tell that story until they die," Mr. Morris said.

❧ Hiroshima Stories

A number of students read and responded to the article "Two Hiroshima Stories," which had been published in the school's magazine, *Hiroshima Signpost: The English Language Monthly*. Written by foreign residents living in Hiroshima, the magazine had a circulation of about five hundred. International School's principal and teacher Walter Enloe wrote the first part of the article, and Swiss educator Gauthier Loffler wrote the second part, one of many articles he wrote on his personal journey of peacemaking in Hiroshima.

Mushroom Cloud

> "It is hard for me to believe that almost three decades have passed since my wife and I arrived in Hiroshima for the first time, but I have no doubt that what I learned there has affected everything I have done or felt since. Hiroshima, along with its pain, offers a special kind of illumination."
>
> —Robert Jay Lifton,
> from preface to *Death in Life: Survivors of Hiroshima*

The old Puritan world view saw the child as evil incarnate: innately unruly and spoiled. As with witches, so with children, the devil and his works had first to be searched for and discovered and then beaten out of them. However, as far as I, a teacher in an international school, am concerned, it is not the child that is dangling by a thread over the fires of hell; it is me. Teachers everywhere mediate between opposing viewpoints on curriculum content, in regard to subjects such as evolution and human sexuality. But teachers in the international environment must face the additional problem of parental worries about this very environment. What do we emphasize most: the culture of the host country, or the history of our home country? How can we teach inches and feet in a world almost all metric?

In the almost continuous discussions of what it means to teach in an international school, ethnocentrism and "adulto" centrism also prevail. The fact that the school is in Hiroshima City, which is also a potent symbol, compounds the issues further, with a parent body often disagreeing over the atomic bombing and the nature and goal of peace education.

A perfect example of how two mature, reasonable adults can disagree about questions of human value is the debate over nuclear proliferation. Please do not misunderstand me. I am a teacher partly because of the dynamic human issues which can be raised in the school environment and which encourage children and adults to have reasonable arguments. Hiroshima International School is an excellent place to have such heated discussions. Issues such as gum chewing and caffeine drinks are a thing of the past; expectations for homework are perennial. But one very special and highly delicate issue has raised its head at two opposite ends of the globe, which nevertheless are forever historically linked. The issue concerns the mushroom cloud. In both Hiroshima and Richland (in the State of Washington, USA), idealistic and thought-provoking adolescents are wrestling with the important question of what their sports team should be called. Unlike the "eating on the bus" issue, this one has serious socio-political overtones for both communities.

Hiroshima International School has a problem because we have a junior high ball team that has played games without a mascot. The original members of the team want to establish a name and a tradition. In Richland, Washington, the team does have a name, which has great support among its community, but which also has thousands of opposing voices throughout the rest of the United States. Richland High is the home of the Bombers, whose emblem is the mushroom cloud formed in 1945 over Hiroshima. Richland is the home of the Hanford Nuclear Reservation, the major employer of the town's 30,000 residents, and the primary developer of the nuclear weapons industry in the wartime days of the Manhattan Project (the code name for the development of the nuclear bomb used on Hiroshima). The Beavers changed their name to the Bombers at a time when the town was gushing with pride over its role in developing the atomic bombs that ended World War II. Today, most of the townspeople think that a campaign by a small group of high-schoolers to change the emblem of the mushroom cloud is nothing less than an affront to civic pride, if not to historical fact. The mushroom symbol is everywhere, outlined on the floor tile of the entrance hall to the school, on a sign towering over the football field, on letter jackets and high school rings, and on the business card of every faculty member. It's a tradition.

In Hiroshima and Richland, kids are asking, "What's in a name?" While Richland has its Atomic Bowling Lanes and a main thoroughfare, Nuclear Lane, Hiroshima hasn't been sacrosanct about the concept of heiwa, or peace. In the city, we have the Peace Mannequin Company, Peace Plastic Surgery, the Peace Service Station, and even Peace Pachinko and Pinball Hall, not to mention Peace Park. For months, the HIS (Hiroshima International School) kids have been searching for a name, a symbol for their team, and as expected from imaginative pubescent thinkers, they've come up with a litany of strange suggestions. The Nosepickers and the Cockroaches were initial gags; the Fighting Cranes and the Seahawks got some play, only to be subjugated by the No-names, the Losers, and the Hunks in Steel (or Satin). Inevitably rather serious debate and propaganda for the A-Bombs, the Nukeheads, and the LB's (Little Boys) were heard.

I share the non-Puritanical notion about kids expressed by Jim, an English teacher of Richland, "Our kids are good kids. They're not warmongers. But there is almost a mob reaction going on here. Our job is to make them think."

Now our Critical Thinking class has a real, genuine concern and not the moral and social simulations we often act out. After lots of discussion, most of our students agreed with the feelings of Richland's baseball coach, Scott Woodward. He remembered the year before when a group of Japanese high school students toured Richland and saw the local kids wearing their letter jackets with the mushroom cloud. Trying to explain the emblem to the Japanese students he said, "Left me feeling like I was standing outside without a fig leaf on." The HIS kids thought it would be offensive to Hiroshima residents to walk Hondori with a nuclear cloud imprinted on their sweatshirts, but then again, some argued it's just a symbol. They talked to Mr. Yaguchi, our beloved bus driver and a bomb victim. He thought the mushroom cloud emblem would be fine if it had three or four doves sitting on top, like partridges in a pear tree. The Dove Bombers?

I'll never forget in 1970 playing in a losing soccer game at the University of Miami before screaming fans yelling "Kill 'em, Nuke 'em, Kill 'em, Nuke 'em." How did they know the Florida defensive back was from Hiroshima? Perhaps I glowed in the dark. No, "nuke 'em" had become a battle cry for the gridirons of the atomic age. Forty years ago the majestic mushroom cloud signified to those Richland folk the proud end to a terrible war. Today it embodies a symbol of world destruction. We children of the nuclear age will proceed to choose a name, perhaps a wild animal, for our team. Personally I have hope we will choose the image of a dark, dead globe in the throes of nuclear winter. Then we would call our team, and all of us, The Losers.

30 Years Old on Boys' Day

A monument free of intrigues in the midst of the Peace Park celebrates its 30th birthday this coming May 5, Boys' Day. A party will be held for the weather-worn concrete statue with a child holding an iron paper crane on top of it. The monument's story inspires children all over the world to fold millions of paper cranes every year. The origami inspired by Genbakunokomnozo produces so many small, colorful paper birds that all the monuments in the Peace Park can be decorated all through the year with newly made bundles of folded paper. Day by day, red- and blue-dressed tourist guides narrate the statue's story, retold in different ways: the story of Sadako Sasaki, who died of leukemia at the age of twelve, ten years after she had been exposed to the atomic bomb radiation on August 6, 1945.

Monkey

Sadako's house stood along the Hakushima streetcar line, two hundred yards north of Hatchobori. On the morning of August 6, 1945, she was playing outdoors. Her parents, busy in their barber shop, could not keep an eye on their firstborn daughter for a while and Sadako was exposed to radiation. She wasn't hurt by burns, nor were her parents, who rushed out of the crushed and burning home just in time. Relatives in Kyushu were able to lend money to rebuild the barber shop. Soon Sadako-chan acquired a healthy sister and brother. Because her elder brother often teased her, she somehow lost cheerfulness early, clenching her teeth while helping her mother as much as she could.

In school Sadako was popular for her running abilities, and on sports days, held twice a year, she made a name for herself by helping to win the popular end-of-the-day class relays. Her cheering classmates called her "monkey," which seemed to fit this girl perfectly, for she could run as if she were leaping through empty space. Sadako felt uneasy sharing the joy of having won loudly and in public. She enjoyed singing on her own. Often on her way home from school she heard herself singing a song from her childhood, her lips chanting: "Moon is shining, night is wonderful, come sing and dance with me, come, come, come."

During November 1954, Sadako caught a cold and developed an enlarged lymph node. The node was investigated by the Atomic

Bomb Casualty Commission on Hijiyama Hill. Her parents had brought her up the hill to foreign doctors, although the research institute had incurred some hostility for its policy of examination without treatment. Sadako's parents learned that their daughter had a fatal disease. Before sending her to the Red Cross Hospital, her parents presented Sadako with her first kimono, sadly symbolizing her entry into maidenhood. The present was expensive, but the bills for medical treatment almost ruined the family.

Paper Cranes

In the hospital she was rarely visited by her classmates, as rumors circulated that atomic bomb illnesses were contagious. Not knowing about her deteriorating health, she occasionally ran through the hospital corridors to visit other children and play with them. Sadako saw one of her playmates, a younger girl, dying of leukemia. She got a shock: "Will that happen to me too?" Her mother continued to console her, buying her rice cakes and candies. "You'll soon get better," Sadako-chan often heard from a mother withholding her tears.

It's not certain who told Sadako about the meaning of folding cranes. According to an old superstition, folding paper cranes helps to cure diseases. The real crane often serves as a symbol of love and long life. Sadako had started to fold paper cranes when her condition restricted her to bed. Although she soon learned to do it quickly and properly, the paper she used made it a tough task. The bedridden girl made use of the grease-proofed paper used to wrap her medicine since at that time pills were not yet common and cheap enough for everybody.

She fixed on the saying that folding 1,000 paper cranes would make one's wish come true. And Sadako-chan continued to fold them long after the goal of 1,000 had been met. However, she suddenly refused medication for her steadily worsening pain because "it will slow down the healing process." Her death on October 15, 1955, was reported in all the local papers: "Another child died of leukemia, the atomic bomb disease." After her funeral, a private chart was found on which Sadako had written down the changing numbers and percentage of red and white corpuscles in her blood. The discovery that she had more than a presentiment of her young and seemingly useless death shocked many adults in the face of the determination of a twelve-year-old girl so bitterly fighting for her life. Her bereaved family still had to pay the bills for Sadako's transfusions for a long time. It forced the family to move to a smaller and less expensive house. Is it meaningless to fold paper cranes, remembering Sadako?

The Janitor

Among those people who knew about Sadako Sasaki's existence only from the newspapers covering her brave death was twenty-six-year-old Ichiro Kawamoto. As the mid-fifties politically were a time of intense ideological warfare that forced people apart while curbing almost all peace movements in Hiroshima as well as elsewhere, Kawamoto deliberately decided to pursue his own peace activities. Quitting his regular job and becoming a day laborer, he made himself find time to help poor hibakusha. The young man born in Peru, South America, often visited families who had lost children due to the atomic bomb's aftereffects.

The meeting with Mrs. Sasaki planted the idea in Kawamoto's mind to render Sadako's death a little bit meaningful by asking her former classmates to start a campaign for a monument for all children victimized by a war they had no responsibility for. After the children had agreed, Kawamoto asked Sadako's school principal to give official support. The poorly dressed day laborer was turned down, for he had no clear plan. Through leafleting and sending letters telling Sadako's story and asking for support, the children gradually received a lot of money. Seeing the campaign burgeoning, the school principal took over the responsibility for the project, which was renamed "Campaign for the Children's Peace Monument." The successful story and the many newspaper articles led as-yet-undecided supporters to join the dream Kawamoto Ichiro had first. The Sasaki family did its best to give their time to the various groups that asked the barber family for cooperation. By the end of 1956, enough money had been raised to appoint a famous Tokyo art professor to sculpt the monument, and the unveiling ceremony took place on May 5, 1958, followed by a film company shooting a semi-documentary about Sadako's life and her brave classmates erecting her a monument.

At the party thanking the movie makers, the unemployed Kawamoto, who had mainly given support to the Sasaki family during the three-year statue campaign, brought forward the idea of building a new children's peace group independent of dogma and without any political affiliations. Thus, Orizurunokai, The Paper Crane Club, was founded, and up to today members continue to visit and help forgotten hibakusha while also sharing the responsibility for folding paper cranes, which have become an international symbol for children wishing peace.

The Sasaki family now lives in Kyushu. They left Hiroshima in 1959 since the campaign had made many people wonder about a family who apparently capitalized on the death of their daughter. How else, they asked, than by being rich, is it possible to become so popular? When the Sasakis left Hiroshima they also had to give their second son up for adoption to more successful relatives.

Ichiro Kawamoto still lives in town, now a janitor at Jogakuin Junior High School. Among the many other activities he started was the successful campaign to preserve the Atomic Bomb Dome, since in the sixties many people wanted the crippled building to disappear forever.

When I recently visited the thirty-year-old A-bombed children's statue, halfway between the well-preserved former Prefectural Industrial Promotion Hall and the Cenotaph, inside the Peace Park, a blue-dressed tourist guide explained that the red and black and white "V" on the statue would stand for "victims." For me, it was like hearing "victory" and from far away I heard Sadako-chan's voice, whispering: "Why did they make war on me?"

"So that's how come we have our school's mascot. I never knew that," Isaac said.

"Yes you did," Dean replied. "You just don't remember."

"Of course we were younger then. It didn't matter to us," Mai added.

"It matters now," Isaac stated. "It definitely does."

"We'll be meeting Mr. Kawamoto soon," Emily reminded them.

Kim declared, "He really is a hero."

"So are all the students of the Club," Mai added.

"I don't know if he would call himself a hero," said Isaac thoughtfully.

"Maybe that's what makes him one," Dean said. "Like my grandfather."

"And like my grandparents," Isaac said. "And Yaguchi-san. Doves on a nuke cloud. What a strange symbol."

"Of hope," Raina said. "It's our only way out—to have doves cover up the atomic clouds and make them disappear forever."

"Forever and forever, amen," Dean whispered.

"You'll see," Raina said. "Sadako's monument sits in an oasis of peace."

12

Life Ain't Fair

In the art-and-craft room Kino and Curtis were working on a large mural some four by four meters showing a mushroom cloud covered with doves, based on Mr. Yaguchi's idea. He still had nightmares of burning corpses and the firebomb. He was only sixteen at the time and now forty years later he still dreamed. The upper level had decided in the past week to be the "Seahawks," not the "Bombers." Seahawks were everywhere in the area and there was no need to offend people by calling themselves bombers. The mural was not for the basketball team; it was to hang in the school entrance with posters in English and Japanese. Curtis and Kino presented it at class meeting. Their poster had the words of Pope John Paul II when he spoke in Hiroshima and Nagasaki. Curtis read it aloud:

> *"Hear my voice, for it is the voice of the victims of all wars and violence among individuals and nations.*
>
> *Hear my voice, for it is the voice of all children who suffer and will suffer when people put their faith in weapons and war.*
>
> *Hear my voice when I beg you to instill into the hearts of all*

human beings the wisdom of peace, the strength of justice. and the joy of fellowship.

Hear my voice, for I speak for the multitudes in every country and in every period of history who do not want war and are ready to walk the road of peace.

Hear my voice and grant insight and strength so that we may always respond to hatred with love, to injustice with total dedication to justice, to need with the sharing of self, to war with peace.

Oh God, hear my voice and grant unto the world your everlasting peace."

—Pope John Paul II, Hiroshima and Nagasaki, 1981

No one said a thing at first. Then Kino spoke up: "Well done, mate."

"It really is powerful," Mai said. "I remember that day so well now."

Kim and Raina then presented to the class the other poster, in fire engine red with black lettering, which had a quote from the book *Hibakusha* that Kino had translated into English:

"Hiroshima is not simply a fact of history. It is a warning and an admonition to the present, when the danger of nuclear war dominates everything. Some say that we are now only three minutes from nuclear conflict. We have to ensure that the hands approaching midnight on the clock are put back by five minutes, ten minutes—no, rather, we must prevent nuclear war.

"The road to the abolition of nuclear weapons is long and steep. This means that we must speak out all the more loudly and put all the more strength into our efforts. The strength of one person is slight, perhaps, but no one is perfectly powerless. It is my conviction that peace will be built through the efforts of individuals. It is now that the strength of the individual is needed. From one person to two, from two to three, from three to four: with perseverance, slowly but surely the ring of peace will be widened."

—Akihiro Takahashi, "The Turning Point"

At the class meeting discussion inevitably focused on the readings of the past week. Johann started it off by saying, "The more I read, the more I know and the less I understand."

"What exactly are you talking about?" Raina asked.

"The whole question of Hiroshima," he replied. "Should the bomb have been used?"

Others joined in.

"If it was used to frighten the Soviet Union," Junior said.

"If it hadn't been used, a million Allied soldiers would have died, along with millions of civilians," Rand commented.

"It was used because President Truman was hateful of oriental peoples," Janelle declared.

"The Japanese were already defeated and would surrender in a few months," said Mai.

"They would never give up, so it was the only way. Is that true?" Raina asked.

"Many American scientists were against it, including Einstein, the father of it all," said Emily.

"The Germans were trying to build a bomb," Kim interjected.

"So were the Japanese. At Kyoto University," Johann added.

"The truth is stranger than fiction," Isaac said. "Questions, questions! Where are the answers and the truth?"

"Somewhere in between, under and around," Kim said.

"Remember Mr. Cousins's essay in the *Saturday Review* the week after August 6,1945?" Johann reminded them. "Remember it was titled, 'Modern Man Is Obsolete.'"

"Yes," Mai said, "It raised the fundamental question, Are people born violent? Is it part of our inheritance to be aggressive, to kill, to hurt others, or is it learned in our families and cultures?"

"Might it be both, some of both our natural self from our genes and some from our environment?" Kim asked.

"Oh, we are such human animals," Isaac said. "Maybe if we put the adults who would want to destroy the world into a spaceship and send them to Mars."

"Too close," Emily said. "Maybe Pluto."

"Remember that discussion we had about how much and how little progress we have made the past two hundred years in human rights and freedoms, about how far we've come and how far we have to go to create a just world ?" Mai asked.

"Life ain't fair," Emily said.

"Think about what people looking back two hundred years from now are going to say about this world today—immature, inhuman, stupid!" Isaac said.

"We've got a United Nations Declaration of Human Rights without human responsibilities," Mai added. "And until we take being human seriously from the day a person is born, things are going to improve ever so slowly, if they do."

"My mom said something the other day I've thought about a lot," Dean reflected. "She said if the world was destroyed by atomic warfare and all the humans were killed, there would still be Nature, but she would have no consciousness of herself because we're not part of it."

"Why are we humans so stupid? All of us!" Raina said.

No one answered.

Peacemakers in Peace Park

The bus crossed the Aioi bridge, which led to the hub of the city, often described as the "Venice of Asia" because of its labyrinth of waterways and bridges. The bus parked in front of the Children's Monument, in the middle of a small plaza. Around the base of the monument, which from a distance looked like a thirty-foot-tall concrete rocketship, were millions of cranes. Perched on top of this missile of peace was a brass statue of a girl holding high a crane, and from it hung a rainbow jetstream of thousands of cranes that were tied to the statue's bronze bell.

Most of the cranes hanging on or piled around the statue were gathered into strands of a thousand cranes. Each strand had a small, lettered banner with the donor's name, address or school, and class. Beginning in elementary school throughout Japan each year, students took one- to four-day field trips. From grades five to twelve almost every student in Japan visits Hiroshima at least once. And it is mainly these visiting students who bring the cranes to Peace Park. Now Kim and Mai placed their thousand cranes. These were the cranes that had been folded from the paper lantern found on Miyajima beach, cranes from the International School Language Club, and cranes folded on Friendship Night at the World Friendship Center.

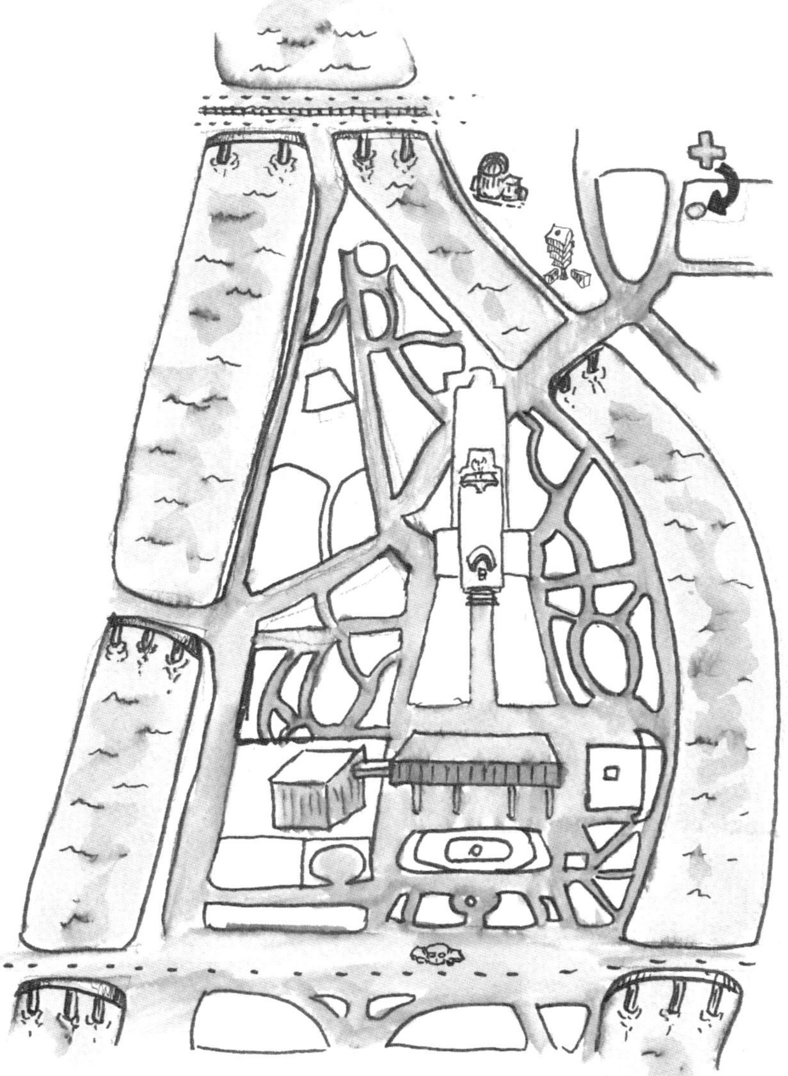

At the monument this morning were a group of seventh graders from Okayama, which was an hour by "bullet train" from Hiroshima. They were dressed alike, the boys in black pants, white shirts, and jackets, and the girls in dark, pleated skirts, white blouses, and dark jackets.

Most school uniforms were similar and could be distinguished only by school pins and name badges. The students jockeyed with each other and surged toward the International School students, laughing and smiling and teasing and yelling out the bits of English they had learned in their first year of studying a foreign language.

"Haro, haro."

"How are you?"

"Fine, thank you, and you?"

Then some of the foreign students replied in Japanese.

"Ohayo gozaimasu? Ikagadesuka?"

The Japanese students were at first shocked and then thrilled. These foreign students spoke Japanese! Soon photographs were being taken and autographs signed. This was not unusual for the International School students.

They enjoyed their fifteen seconds of fame and said goodbye as Dean asked two of the students in Japanese, "Why do you come here?"

"It's our field trip this year," a girl said.

"But why come here?" Dean asked again.

"It is the choice of the school," she replied.

"We bring our cranes," another student added.

"We want peace to always be here," the girl said.

"So do we," Dean said. "So do we."

❧ Peacemaker

Mr. Morris and Dean walked toward an older Japanese man who was sweeping near the monument. They all bowed deeply and smiled. The man was Mr. Kawamoto, the peace activist and janitor who had started the 1000 crane movement. Dean called the other students over and asked them to read the article about Mr. Kawamoto he had prepared and handed out on the bus. It was titled "Peacemaker of Cranes."

Mr. Kawamoto was Japanese, but he was born in Peru. His parents died when he was twelve, and he moved back to Hiroshima to live with relatives. He was sixteen the day of the atomic bombing. Later he worked for the electric company, but when Hiroshima began rebuilding, he gave up his job and became a peace activist and school janitor.

Mr. Kawamoto was a family friend of Sadako Sasaki, and after her death he came up with the idea of building a children's monument to commemorate all the children who died from the atomic bombing. Through the monument, students from around the world would appeal to the adult leaders and parents to work for peace. Mr. Kawamoto's idea grew into the Folded Crane Club and then a nationwide Youth Movement for Peace. His original idea was expressed in a leaflet that he helped students in Sadako's class write. The leaflet led thousands of children around the world to contribute to funds for the monument.

In the biography of Sadako that Dean's father and mother were now translating into English, there was a copy of the leaflet. Two thousand copies of it were delivered to the Junior High School Principals Conference held in Hiroshima in November 1955, two weeks after Sadako's death. It read:

Let's Build a Monument for the Children of the A-Bomb

We wish to announce our desire to the principals gathered from all over the country.

Sadako Sasaki-san, a close friend of ours, died on October 25, of A-bomb disease. We knew her since we were small. We studied and played together and enjoyed each other's company. An innocent child, Sadako-san suddenly fell ill in January this year and died after suffering nine long months. We cannot help but feeling sad for Sadako-san, who knew the A-bomb in her heart and died. But since there is nothing we can do about it, at least we wish to console the spirits of all the children who have died in the same way by building a statue for the children of the A-bomb.

Please make our appeal to our friends at junior high schools all over the country and win their support. We want this message to be told to junior high students by you, their principals. We came here especially to request this.

—Hiroshima Municipal Noboricho Junior High School 7th graders and all the classmates of the late Sadako Sasaki

---

"Thank you for coming today. It is good to see you here," Mr. Kawamoto said. "It is important, your work of studying the place you live, even if for a short time. I know this too. Sadako would be proud to know your quest for understanding and your commitment to peacemaking. It's so good of your teacher and your principal Dr. Enloe to support you. You know, I knew your principal when he was your age and he would come and visit the Peace Park on Saturdays, riding his bike down to the river, and sometimes we would talk." He stopped and turned to the monument.

"And I am happy to see your garlands of cranes and to

note for the first time an English and Japanese banner from Students of the International School of Hiroshima. It reads: *In Peace.* I and my friends, young and old, have been caring for this sacred place each week for the past twenty-seven years. We have had many foreign visitors to whom we have presented the peace crane. And occasionally I have seen cranes from other places—usually, I think, placed here by your school. But today is such a special time for you guest citizens of the International City of Peace to make such a pilgrimage."

Everyone was quiet, mesmerized by this humble man who was anxious to return to his grave responsibility, the cleaning of the monument and plaza, where each week he removed the paper birds of peace that had been tattered and soiled by the wind and rain, weathered by the sun, and whose time it was to return to the dust from which its trees had originally sprung.

"Before you continue I must show you a message from all the children who initiated and participated in this project and to which you may now join." The group walked to the back of the monument, and Kawamoto-san kneeled and rubbed his hands gently over the copper plate in a respectful incantation. The plate was inscribed in Japanese: To comfort the souls of our brothers and sisters who died because of the A-bomb, and to appeal to the world for peace, the elementary, junior high, and senior high students of Hiroshima, with the help of friends all over the country, have joined hands and worked together to build this monument. May 5, 1958, The Hiroshima Children and Students Association for the Creation of Peace.

"So continue your journey," said Mr. Kawamoto, "for

peace in your lives and the world. This monument belongs to you too." And then he turned and resumed his sweeping and cleaning. Silently the students walked through the park, past the Mound of the Souls—the thousands of unknown people whose ashes were buried here, and past the Cenotaph, which held the names of the known who had died from the bombing. They walked across the main plaza through a rippling sea of cooing doves and at last stood in front of the museum.

❧ Under the Museum

They were to meet back here in thirty minutes. The museum, a repository of artifacts and photographs of that fateful day, was perched on pillars some twenty feet off the ground. Most of the students had been here before with their family or on a class trip. All visitors to Hiroshima were drawn to this place. From here students could investigate the museum's record of the past, visit the Pope's Monument in the Peace Culture Foundation, or buy bread crumbs to feed the doves. Underneath the museum, rockers rocked and a young man in a wheelchair collected signatures from people to oppose the testing of nuclear weapons. Around the museum lovers and friends and families and visitors wandered and wondered or bought bread crumbs to feed the doves.

Junior noticed the man in the wheelchair and wondered aloud, "Do you think he could be a bomb victim?"

"No, no," Johann whispered. "He's too young. Maybe a mutant."

"That's inappropriate," Junior said.

"Hey guys," Raina interrupted, "If you knew anything, you could tell he has CP like me."

They stopped. Cerebral palsy—they hadn't thought of that. She looked at both of them and then quietly said, "We're all bomb victims. Everyone of us is disabled."

"I didn't mean..." Johann tried to say something, wishing he could explain that the joking masked his fears that could be seen in the horrors upstairs and now were memories and vignettes that he could never erase from his mind.

"No, it's not about that," Raina said. "I understand. It's about us."

❧ Powerful Places

As Mr. Enloe came down the stairs from the bowels of the museum of death, he acknowledged the young man collecting signatures. They talked for a minute and then Mr. Enloe beckoned the students over.

"This is Mr. Kawaguchi and he is a peacemaker. He lives at the Grace Rehabilitation Center, which Mr. Ihara and my father developed years ago as the first institution for disabled adults. Several hundred people live there and are productive in their work and lives."

"Could I visit there?" Raina asked.

"Sure. They would welcome you, Raina. And all of you."

"Where is it?"

"In Tadanoumi on the Inland Sea. Raina, Mr. Ihara, a Christian minister, has muscular dystrophy and over the years has given up his crutches and wheelchair to be carried by his family."

"When you were interviewed with us last summer, didn't you tell that story?" Dean asked.

"Yes," replied Mr. Enloe. "My father and Mr. Ihara

worked to create a church and then the center. A young boy in America nicknamed Flip Lyons was dying of leukemia and as an act of love and faith he gave all his money for these projects and there is a plaque in his memory at the church."

"Another oasis of peace!" exclaimed Dean.

"Yes, both the church and the center are, because they are examples of places full of the spirit of love and compassion and giving. Before the center was built and became a national model, disabled and handicapped people were cared for at home, isolated from the public, and without any way to meet other people with similar needs and aspirations. Oases of peace. Powerful places."

❧ Hibakusha Shock

Ms. Matsubara stood at the entrance to the library in the Peace Culture building. She had stood there tens upon tens of time noting the faces, some smiling, some sad, some forlorn. Almost everyone wore a mask, trying to hide their concern. Many glanced at her. She smiled graciously and bowed as each student walked in to the meeting area. Often she caught someone glancing again at her and the disfigured side of her face. She no longer tried to hide it; a bit of powder seemed to blend the scars into the rest of her. She was a nervous woman, full of expectation and delight.

For many years she had told her story about August 6 and its aftermath, of the day—her fourteenth birthday—when the world caught fire and burned. And she had been terribly burned and had suffered through many surgeries.

Over the years she had become a committed peace activist, only recently moving from outside these walls to tell

her story. She had just returned from her first peace pilgrimage to the United States and Europe where she visited schools and churches, bringing the peace message of Hiroshima.

Time after time she told her story. This was the first time for her to meet with a group of foreign students, and most important, children who lived in or near Hiroshima. On the phone the day before, Ms. Matsubara had talked with Dr. Enloe, whom she had known from their work together at the World Friendship Center.

"Do you want them to experience story 1, 2, or 3?" she said.

"Which do you prefer?" he asked.

"My heart tells me number 3. They are still young and are full of their feelings of confusion and angst. Only one or two will cry outwardly. More inside."

"Whatever you feel. These are wonderful young people on a powerful quest to understand themselves and their world and its potential future."

She began with a slide show from the Hiroshima Nagasaki Study Committee that could be purchased in the museum "gift" shop. It showed picture after picture of the emotional, physical, and social devastation of people and the city. Indelibly marked in each person's mind were the burning bodies and terribly scarred flesh of other human beings.

"I was hurt in bombing and was very sick," said Ms. Matsubara. "I went to school that day to help weed our gardens of onions and radishes. Then came the thunderbolt and I was pinned under a building. When I woke I was in a makeshift hospital. I was covered in gauze and had ointment on my body's burns. Most people seemed dead around me. I was on a pallet on the floor of a hall with hundreds of hurt people everywhere. Every day the place was full of the dead. I am fortunate, for most hospitals and doctors and nurses were destroyed and killed. My parents were killed too, but I did not know this at the time. Only that I was there with no pain medicines and only a rice ball and water each day.

"For weeks I lay there and replayed in my mind what I had seen and heard and sometimes I couldn't tell if the horrors were dreams or memories of what really happened. But they were so incredibly real. It was terribly sad for so long. Then one day my mother's sister walked right by me. She was visiting a neighbor. I cried out, 'Auntie, Auntie.' She came back every day after that and then took me to her place. But it took more than two months, because my wounds were so deep and the skin grew back in such twisted and scarred ways. You can see the results, can't you? Look at my hands."

She stretched out her hands to the group. Then she continued, "And look closely at my face. Behind this mask of makeup can you make out the disfigurements of me?" Then she began a rhythmic incantation:

"People on fire...People naked...People with their skin peeling off...People corpses...People ghosts...And the sick and the dying? There were no painkillers, no medicines, only the crying and whimpering. Who remembered us? Who cared for us? We were the dead and dying. The walking dead."

She continued, "Then later I went to my aunt's place, where the house had burned down and under a piece of tin and wooden board she had fashioned a cave where we lived the next three years. We were to have all kinds of ailments. I lost all my hair—everywhere on my body. My teeth ached and my gums bled. We had A-bomb sickness. It was mysterious but real. We had the malaise of just feeling weak and weary and wishing for death. It is a nagging weariness all the way down into your bone marrow. It won't go away. Sometimes you are dizzy. Sometimes your digestive system turns to stone or becomes a river and goes crazy with loss of blood.

"So you see, you grow up to live this in Hiroshima. As the place becomes outwardly peaceful. Buildings are built on the rubble and gardens planted and people go on with their lives. Skyscrapers and neon signs light up the night. And yet inside you are dark and this sense of dread and doom covers you in darkness. I am dying. We're getting cancers. Years later. Blood cancers like Sadako. You know you're going to get the A-bomb diseases from the radiation. You know you are a part of the great experiment of the twentieth century, maybe of all time. Not just an instant sickness and death but one that eats at you day after day, month after month, year after year."

She paused. Not a sound could be heard in the library.

"Even our own people treat us as untouchables. We are weak. We are tainted. We are worthless. Our own people discriminate against us. And it took years for us to be helped. Rats and guinea pigs in the laboratories are treated royally compared to what has happened to us. We are living dead. Even our government is quick to forget us. Our employers distrust and despise us. Even our neighbors treat us as second-class citizens. This is the terror of Hiroshima and nuclear war.

"Thank you for listening. Today I give you a number 3 story. Number 1 is also the truth but closer and deeper. Then everybody would cry, throw up, and run out of the room. Thank you very much for being here today."

13

Truth Is Stranger Than Fiction

Everyone had gathered for Monday morning meeting. The ritual of welcoming, messages, and making decisions was executed with the normalcy of a Swiss timepiece. The youngest children came to sing a new song they had learned in French. Mai patiently waited her turn. Finally she said, "You won't believe it, but I found it." She waved a handful of papers in the air.

"What did you find?" Kim asked.

"Remember last week we were talking about variations on a story and the whole notion of what is the true story and who owns the story? Well, this weekend my family went to see my brother Jim at Canadian Academy. And I went to the library to do the cross-reference approach we learned. And I found an article called the 'The Thousand Cranes,' written in 1963. That's also the name of Mr. Kawabata's novel for which he won the Nobel Prize in 1968."

"Who wrote the story?" someone asked.

"Betty Jean Lifton. The poet whose poem is over there on the bulletin board. She lived here in 1962 with her husband, the psychiatrist who studied the Hiroshima survivors. His book is called *Death in Life*. We have it here."

"How did you know where to go?"

"One of my 3 x 5 cards has a reference from a book on Hiroshima and child victims of the bomb. I didn't know they had the magazines, but I went to the library and in the stacks they had this literary magazine from the States called *Hornbook* magazine."

"Good detective work."

"What did you learn?"

"Several things," said Mai. "Listen to this. She tells Sadako's story. She says that Sadako lived a mile from the epicenter and that she was very brave in the hospital. Sadako tried to fold a thousand cranes but was only able to fold 964 before she died."

"Another variation on her story," Kim remarked.

"Her book tells about the building of the monument and the movie. Many of the characters were Sadako's friends who then formed the Orizurukai or Folded Crane Club. And they met at Peace Park in a shack where Mr. Kawamoto lived."

"We met him Friday," Kino said. "That was cool."

"Well, one other thing," Mai said. "She had an idea."

"Who?" asked Dean. "Mrs. Lifton? or Sadako? or Eleanor Coerr?"

"No, listen," Isaac said, walking across the room with a book. "Here Eleanor Coerr writes in *Sadako and the Paper Cranes* that she got the idea from a book she read on children of the A-bomb."

"Let's find it!" said Johann.

"I'm sure it's in the library," Isaac stated.

"Does it really matter?" asked Kino.

"The truth? Yes it does!!" declared Mai.

"Why does it matter if she folded 644 or 744 or 10,844?" asked Kino.

"Because," replied Mai.

"Because isn't good enough!" Kino declared.

"Different versions give different perspectives," said Isaac.

"What's really true anyway?" commented Dean.

"We've got an idea too," Kim said.

"Let me read this first," Mai continued. "This is at the end of the story:

> Mrs. Lifton would appreciate ideas from parents, teachers, or any individuals who might know ways in which American children could be reached emotionally, and with the children of Hiroshima, but in their own communities, join in helping the less fortunate, secure in the knowledge that in a world where people love and help each other, there is the possibility of peace. They can learn to fold paper cranes from almost any book of origami, and perhaps they would like to exchange cranes with the children of Hiroshima, or letters or scrapbooks. They might decide to write their feelings to the heads of their countries....They might start a chain of cranes moving from one child to another, the way the chain letters used to move. And perhaps those paper cranes, flying from child to child, city to city, state to state, country to country, would bear the children's desire for peace in the world. I may not know how the children of America will respond, but I do know they will need adults to lead them. They will have to have their Pied Pipers, be they teachers, parents, or ministers, to guide them and inspire them along the way.

"Wait till you hear our idea after Peace Park Friday," Heather said.

"It's exciting," Mia added.

❧ The Bells of Nagasaki

"It's time we talk with some Japanese students in Hiroshima to see what they're doing about remembering Hiroshima and working toward peace," Andrea argued.

"I thought about that too," Mia chimed in, "but they are now older people, all adults."

"No, I don't mean them—like Mr. Tanimoto's kids, KoKo and Ken. We can interview them easily. What I mean are people our age."

"You mean, what are the students at Ushita Junior High doing?" Isaac asked.

"Exactly." Andrea replied. "Look what I found last week in Nagasaki last week. My dad helped me check the English. He helped me write this in Dutch, then English. English is so difficult because you have all of your idioms and words that are spelled the same but sound different or that are spelled different but sound the same. It's a mess," she laughed. Then she handed out her report, "Children's Peacemaking and the Bells of Nagasaki." Andrea had folded her report into booklets, and inside each one she had glued a small paper crane.

Children's Peacemaking and the Bells of Nagasaki

Was it fate? Or divine retribution? Or pure chance? August 9, 1945. Less than three days since the bombing of Hiroshima. The B-29 bomber was headed for the city of Kokura. Nagasaki was the secondary target, but Kokura was too cloudy for the bombardier to see the city. And so it was that Nagasaki became the second city in the history of humankind to be destroyed by an atomic bomb. Seventy thousand people died in a moment, a second, an hour, a day. More than 75, 000 were injured and many were to die from "atomic diseases" in the weeks and months and years to follow. The hypocenter of the bombing, or Ground Zero, was Urakami district, where many of the residents were Christians. Urakami Cathedral, the largest in Asia, was totally destroyed. More than 8,500 of its 10,000 members were killed. Close by was Shiroyama Elementary School. It means Castle (on) Hill School . Most of the children and teachers were killed. In the first grade there were two hundred students. Only three children survived.

When the bomb fell over Nagasaki, it was close to Nagasaki Medical School. Dr. Takashi Nagai was a dean and professor of radiology, a nuclear physicist, and because it was war he also had a military title, head of the Eleventh Medical Corps. The students and teachers in the medical school were divided into teams, and they were assigned to different areas of the city whenever there was an air raid or natural disaster. While the bomb destroyed much of the medical school hospital and injured and killed many of the staff, students, and patients, and while Dr. Nagai was severely cut on the head by glass, his team was able to make it to the Urakami district, where they were to work twenty-four hours a day until each was exhausted and had to rest. After many days, Dr. Nagai made it home to find it destroyed and his wife incinerated; he found only a few of her small bones. His young daughter, Kayano, and son Makoto were living in the countryside with relatives and so were not injured. There he stood at his burned-out home with the cremated remains of his loving wife, exhausted emotionally, mentally drained, and gravely ill with leukemia. At that moment he made a commitment to his family and God that he would work for peace for the future of all children.

Takashi Nagai was born into a medical family that had served for generations as physicians and herbalists for the imperial family. He was an excellent student and could have attended the Imperial University in Tokyo or Kyoto but decided to go to Nagasaki, since it was known for its excellent and unique studies of Western science and medicine. Though Japan was closed for more than 230 years until the mid-nineteenth century, Nagasaki was a port open to trade only with the Dutch and on occasion with the Chinese. Through that opening of a door to the outside world, Japan was able to keep apace to some degree with advances and discoveries in science, technology, global exploration, governance, and individual status. In Nagasaki, Takashi Nagai decided to board with a Christian family living in the Urakami district. The family's daughter, Midori Moriyama, would become his wife. The family was a member of a Christian group known as the "hidden Christians."

Christianity had flourished in the sixteenth century thanks to the influence of Francis Xavier and Portuguese Catholic priests. There were several hundred thousand converts, particularly around Nagasaki. This very "un-Japanese" religion eventually led to a rebellion against the imperial administration, which led to the massacre of thousands of Christians and the closing of Japan in 1636 to all nations except the Dutch, who were Protestants but were more interested in trade (e.g., Chinese silk for Japanese silver) than in saving souls. Christianity was banned, and for several hundred years hundreds of families outwardly lived Buddhist and Shinto lives while secretly practicing their Christian faith. That tradition continues today.

At the time Takashi Nagai became a doctor, he joined the Imperial Army and was assigned to Manchuria. He found a copy of a Catholic catechism, studied intensely, and upon his return to Nagasaki, was baptized, took the name Paul, after St. Paul, and soon after married Midori. He returned to China for a year, then returned to Nagasaki in 1940 and became a professor of medicine. In June 1945 he was diagnosed with leukemia (from his radiology work) and was given three years to live.

In 1946, though obviously weak and sick, Takashi Nagai continued his teaching and studies of the atomic bomb disease.One day he was at the railroad station when he collapsed and had to be carried home by a friend. Confined to bed, Takashi Nagai's condition worsened. He wrote in his book *Leaving These Children Behind*, "From that day to the present the illness has gradually gained momentum. Now I have to rely on other people even to fetch pieces of paper for me. I barely have the strength to look into a microscope, let alone to examine patients. Fortunately, though, my topic of research—atomic bomb disease—is right here in my own body."

In 1948 people began moving into the atomic wasteland in the Urakami district. Dr. Nagai had a shack constructed close to the cathedral. He put two tatami mats (about four square meters) inside. He named it with a sign outside the entrance Nyoko-do (As Yourself Hermitage), after the Christian maxim "Love others as you love yourself." In that tiny space, within reaching distance around his bed were writing paper, brushes, paints, reference books, and daily articles. The other mat was for his children. The cooking area and the bathroom were outside.

In this place Dr. Nagai began writing books and creating paintings as a way to encourage the people of Nagasaki to hope, live, pray, and work together for a better future each day, each hour, each minute. *Nagasaki no Kane* (Bells of Nagasaki) inspired a hit song that is still popular today. It was his first book,written less than a year after the bombing. He was the first in Japan to write about the bomb—the blast, the destruction, medical insights into the symptoms, struggles, and death of the wounded, and how his Christian faith gave him hope, optimism, and an understanding of sacrifice. The U.S. occupation forces banned his book in 1946 but agreed finally in 1949 to its Japanese publication as long as it included an appendix describing Japanese atrocities in the Philippines. The appendix was dropped in the late 1950s when the occupation forces left. What made the *Bells of Nagasaki* so controversial, I think, is not the description of the moments, days, weeks, and months of living with and dying from the atomic bomb. It wasn't all the details of the suffering of civilians or the details of how doctors tried to help patients but didn't know how to treat those with radiation-related diseases (though Dr. Nagai recognized the symptoms because he had many of them himself). The real problem was that he was a deeply religious man. He was a Christian, very un-Japanese to many in an Eastern world of Buddhism and Shintoism. His book tells the story of a person's inner struggle with the destruction and misery of innocent people and belief in a loving God. Dr. Nagai was both witness and victim of this terrible tragedy, and he cries for world peace as the bells of Urakami Cathedral ring for a better future. The whole book is very powerful, but the most moving part for me was the last pages. Let me set up the situation. It is days after the bombing. One of Dr. Nagai's former students, Dr. Ichitaro, returns to Nagasaki, where he finds the city devastated and his wife and five children turned into ashes.

"I have no joy in life," he lamented.

"Who has joy when we've been defeated in war?" I [Dr. Nagai] replied.

"I suppose you're right. Any Japanese could say what I'm saying. The atomic bomb was punishment from heaven. Those who died were evil people; those who survived received a special grace from God. But then, does this mean that my wife and children were evil people?"

"Well, I have a completely different view. In fact, I have the opposite view. The atomic bomb falling on Nagasaki was a great act of Divine Providence. It was a grace from God. Nagasaki must give thanks to God," I said.

"Give thanks?"

Dr. Nagai then gave him the speech he had written as the Christian representative for the funeral service at Urakami Cathedral for the bomb's victims. He might well have titled it with this line from the last page of his book: "The people of Nagasaki prostrate themselves before God and pray: Grant that Nagasaki may be the last atomic wilderness in the history of the world."

"Before this moment there were many opportunities to end the war. Not a few cities were totally destroyed. But these were not suitable sacrifices; nor did God accept them. Only when Nagasaki was destroyed did God accept the sacrifice. Hearing the cry of the human family, He inspired the emperor to issue the sacred decree by which the war was brought to an end. Our church of Nagasaki kept the faith during four hundred years of persecution when religion was proscribed and the blood of martyrs flowed freely. During the war this same church never ceased to pray day and night for a lasting peace. Was it not, then, the one unblemished lamb that had to be offered on the altar of God? Thanks to the sacrifice of this lamb many millions who would otherwise have fallen victim to the ravages of war have been saved. How noble, how splendid was that holocaust of August 9, when flames soared up from the cathedral, dispelling the darkness of war and bringing the light of peace! In the very depth of our grief we reverently saw here something beautiful, something pure, something sublime. Eight thousand people, together with their priests, burning with pure smoke, entered into eternal life. All without exception were good people whom we deeply mourn. Let us give thanks that Nagasaki was chosen for this sacrifice. Let us give thanks that through this sacrifice peace was given to the world and freedom of religion to Japan. May the souls of the faithful departed, through the mercy of God, rest in peace. Amen."

Andrea finished this section of her report and bowed quietly to the group. Silence. Silence.

Silence.

"I had no idea that people would think this way," Emma said.

"How can he see beauty in such suffering? Is it because he is also suffering so much?" Mai asked.

"He is a person with strong beliefs. He lives through his faith," Isaac added.

"I had never thought of the bombing as a holocaust," Alina noted. She and her sister, Raina, were to move to Israel in a few months.

"Would you really be willing to die for a belief?" Niraj asked.

"I would," Johan said, "if I really believed in it. Like dying for your country. Dying to be free like oppressed people around the world have for thousands of years."

"Would you kill to get food?" Mai asked.

"If people were keeping people like children starving I might," Johan exclaimed.

"No. I wouldn't use evil to win over evil," Emma said.

"Let's keep talking about this, but let me finish my report," Andrea said.

Dr. Nagai's other writings included *Seimei no Kawa* (River of Life), *Rozario no Kusari* (The Rosary Chain), and *Kono Ko wo Nokoshite* (Leaving These Children Behind), which became a well-known film. It was the thought of his children losing their mother and soon himself that motivated him to write so prolifically. In *Leaving These Children Behind* he wrote of his children, "I have to postpone the moment when these children become orphans, even by one day or one hour. Even if it is only one minute or one second, I want to reduce the length of time they must suffer loneliness." In the year before his death he was visited by an emissary of the Pope, received a visit from Helen Keller, and finally, in the months before his death, was visited by the emperor and received a commendation from the prime minister. He died June 1, 1950, at age forty-two. His funeral was held in the ruins of Urakami Cathedral.

Many children had lost their parents, and much of Takashi Nagai's income each month went to help neighborhood children with food and clothing. As in Hiroshima and much of Europe and Asia, there were thousands of orphans. Dr. Nagai created a library and named it "Our Book Case," where children could read and play. He lived his philosophy of "love others as you would love yourself." In the last chapter of *Leaving These Children Behind* Dr. Nagai writes from his bed pallet: "From here I can see Makoto preparing to carry away broken roof tiles in a straw basket, and Kayano playing house by herself and using the fragment of an Arita vase to arrange flowers. I wonder how these children will comment on my way of thinking after they grow up. In fifty years' time they will be much older than I am today. Perhaps when they read this book they will sit together and rattle their false teeth, saying things like, 'Dad certainly had a youthful attitude.'"

Andrea stopped reading. "I have not tried to find his children, but if we did I think they would agree that his life has lived on, that his youthful attitude is still alive today in the hearts and minds of children."

"Do you think they still live there?" Isaac asked.

"I'm not sure. Remember Sadako's family moved. Maybe it would be too difficult living in fame because of your father. I have visited each school in Nagasaki and talked with students and teachers. Here is what I learned." Andrea continued to read from her report.

Powerful testimonies to the Nagasaki experience are two collections of children's stories, *In the Sky over Nagasaki* and *Living Beneath the Atomic Cloud*, compiled by Dr. Nagai. These peace readers published in 1949 were later translated with the help of the Nagasaki Appeal Committee by the Wilmington Peace Resource Center in Wilmington, Ohio. This is a Quaker college where Barbara Reynolds retired after living in Hiroshima and founding the World Friendship Center. I found the books at Dr. Nagai's museum and got permission to use them for my report. One of the stories is by Dr. Nagai's daughter, Kayano, who was five at the time of the bombing and age nine when she told this story, "I Hope My Father Can Walk Soon":

My brother and I were staying at a house in Koba near the mountains for safety. When Mother came from Nagasaki to see us, I asked her, "Mama, have you brought my clothes?" "Yes, of course. I've brought a lot of your clothes," she said, patting me on the head. "Come back to Nagasaki when the air raids have finished," she said, and went back to Nagasaki in a hurry. After the atomic bomb was dropped, it was Father who came up to the house in Koba. His ears and his head were bandaged. All of us went down to Nagasaki together after Father's wounds were healed. My house had been large and Mother used to be there, but now I found everything in ashes and nothing remaining. We built a house of tin in the ruins. We put in two rooms. We slept there, but it was so cramped that I was troubled by my brother kicking me. Though our house was completed, Mama didn't come back to us. Now father is sick in bed all day. He can move his hands, but the rest of his body is unable to move. When he goes out, he must be carried on a stretcher. I hope Father can walk soon. Then I'd like to go the mountains hand in hand with my Father, to draw pictures."

"So powerful," Mai said.

"She writes really well," Emma said.

"And so sad," Raina added.

"The image of her going into the mountains with her father is so vivid. And knowing that he never got to walk again makes it even more powerful," Isaac said.

"Let me share parts of another story, the first in the book." Andrea began to read again.

"I Squat down on the Spot where We Cremated Our Mother and Touch the Earth with My Fingers," by Fujio Tsujimoto (then five years old). The survivors piled up wood on the playground and began to cremate the corpses. My brother was burned. Mother was also burned and quickly turned to white bones, which dropped down through the live coals. I cried as I gazed upon the scene. Grandmother was also watching it, praying with a rosary. Grandmother says that we will meet Mother in heaven. As she is old, she may go to heaven before long, but I'm still a child and may not see my sweet-hearted mother for many years. I cannot play with my elder brother or talk to my dear sisters. I am now in the fourth grade at Yamazato Primary School. That playground of terrible memories is now completely cleared and many of my friends are playing there happily. They are quite ignorant of the fact that so many children were killed and cremated in the very place. Even I play with my friends on that playground, but I sometimes unexpectedly remember that awful day. When I do, I squat down on the spot where we cremated our mother and touch the earth with my fingers. When I dig deep in the ground with a piece of bamboo, several pieces of charcoal appear. Looking at the spot for a while, I can dimly see my mother's image in the earth. So when I see someone else treading upon that spot, it makes me very angry. Whenever I go out into the playground, I remember that day. The playground is dear to me, but at the same time I am very sad there. Let me go back to the past once more. Oh, I want my mother, I want my father, I want my brother, I want my sisters. If only they were alive! Grandma goes to church every morning to take part in Mass. She often prays with a rosary and says to me. "Everything is in His Will. Everything will be all right." I wish I had as pure a heart as Grandma.

"I hope I would have his courage," Harold said.

"It's such a sad story," Alina added.

"I don't know how he could do without his grandmother," said Mai.

"I respect him because he's sad about his family, but he doesn't give up," Emma said.

"The playground was used to cremate bodies just like the one at the old school," noted Isaac.

"Probably because they're flat and open space," Raina explained.

"I respect him and his grandmother," added Johann. "He's sad but alive. She has such strong faith to believe things will be better."

"What would you do?" Isaac asked. "Would you give up or go on living?"

"I would do everything to stay alive," Serene said. "I wonder if we can find any of them today. Dr. Nagai's daughter must be fifty years old. I wonder if she would talk with us."

"Maybe," Andrea said. "Let's try when some of you come to visit me in Nagasaki." Then she continued her report with information about Nagasaki schools.

There were three schools within a kilometer radius of the hypocenter, or Ground Zero (detonation point of the atomic bomb). One was Fuchi Citizen's Junior High School, 1,500 meters from the hypocenter, which officially had more than 1,400 students and some fifty teachers. But all of the students were working in factories in place of older teenagers who had been drafted into the military. Most of the teachers had become work supervisors. The children at Yamazato and Shiroyama Elementary Schools, 700 meters and 500 meters from Ground Zero, had been sent home for their "safety." Instantly in the moments of the explosion, the whole area was changed into an inferno that turned most buildings into rubble and created a blackened, leveled field as far as you could see. Of the 1,400 students in this school district fewer than seventy-five survived. Several years later the schools were rebuilt. One history of the time explains, "Peace education was begun at these schools, which had sacrificed so much, to help ensure the horror war and the tragedy of the atomic bombing would never again be repeated. The peace education efforts initiated by teachers just after the war have been passed on down to the present, and peace education continues today, centered on the schools that were bombed."

Teachers nurture the growth of "seeds of peace consciousness" by helping children understand that peacemaking begins with each of us; the first steps in understanding the tragedy of the atomic bomb and the importance of peace is for each person to get along with others. Understanding peace in daily life includes tolerance and cooperation with others, conflict resolution without fighting, dealing with "ijime" or bullying, kindness to animals, and growing and caring for plants. Teachers emphasize "teaching others what we have learned" rather than "learning what is taught." Teachers see their job as helping kids become ambassadors for peace.

Shiroyama Elementary reopened in 1948. Beginning in 1951, a peace ceremony has been held on the ninth day of each month as a way of remembering August 9, 1945, and as part of the school peace program in honor of Dr. Nagai. The peace curriculum is known as the "Takashi Nagai approach to peace." On the fiftieth anniversary of the bomb, the school unveiled its peace monument. The monument was chosen by vote of the student body from many models the students made. The monument was about a meter tall and consisted of two hands holding three interconnected rings symbolizing boundless hope, an open heart, and deep love. The fiftieth anniversary of the bombing, 1995, became an opportunity for the school to adopt the slogan "Peace from Shiroyama," signifying that the school should become a source of inspiration for peacemaking. The school has produced a "Shiroyama Peace Map" and created around the school grounds five areas as part of its "Shiroyama Peace Zone Project" to promote feelings, images, and thoughts related to peace: "Peace Entrance Zone," "Relaxation Zone," "Atomic Bomb Study Zone," the "Nature Zone," and the "Prayer Zone." Students have made signboards with written explanations and illustrations in each zone, and older students serve as guides or docents.

At Yamazato Elementary School there is a small hill within the school grounds on top of which sits a stone monument known as the "Memorial for Those Children." It is a memorial to the dead children. It was an idea of Dr. Nagai and was built using the royalties from the book *Living Beneath the Atomic Cloud: Testimony of the Children of Nagasaki*, compiled by Dr. Takashi Nagai in 1945. This school's peace program is also based upon Dr. Nagai's love and approach to peace. The school maintains a peace exchange program with the elementary school Dr. Nagai attended, Iiseki Elementary School, in Mitoya, Shimane Prefecture. Once every two years on August 9, students from Iiseki visit Yamazato. They take part in the peace ceremony, play games, and have discussions and a special dinner in the school gym. All of the students at Yamazato keep "peace notebooks" from grade one through grade six, in which they write observations, comments, and essays and create drawings around the theme of peacemaking. When they graduate, their notebooks are bound together and are given back to the students as keepsakes. The school also has a Children's Memorial Hall, a museum of the school and its peacemaking efforts, that is open year round to the public.

Most of Shiroyama's graduates attend Fuchi Junior High School, so the peace education program is a continuation of their peace studies begun in first grade. Peace education is centered on the work of the "Peace Committee," a group of volunteer students who organize various program and events including the monthly "Peace Assembly" on the ninth day of every month. The ceremony is held in front of the school's monument, "Sparkling Life," and includes an offering of flowers, a moment of silence to remember the past, and a pledge to strive for peace without nuclear weapons. One teacher told me that "The emphasis at all the Nagasaki schools is on individual concern. Peace is not forced. It is grown in individual hearts through community work in part. Our goal is to promote informed discussion and debate that respects individual opinion and thought in an atmosphere where reasonable people can often disagree."

"This is great information Andrea," Mai exclaimed. "It helps us have a big picture of Hiroshima and Nagasaki together."

"I agree," Johann added. "We always think Hiroshima and forget Nagasaki."

"Maybe Nagasaki is not only just as important as Hiroshima. Maybe it's more important because it was the last place," Mia thought out loud.

"So far," Junior said.

"Never again. Never," Mai said. "These students are great role models. Each school is an oasis of peace."

Raina's sister, Alina, suggested, "Let's do the peace book idea. Maybe we can call them peace notebooks."

"Okay. Great idea, Alina," Emma exclaimed. "Andrea, let's take a field trip to Nagasaki and visit these schools."

Raina said, "Can we all stay at your house, Andrea?"

"Sure. We would be like hobbits, with all of us sleeping in a Japanese rabbit hutch. Really, that's how small our apartment is."

"I bet we could sleep in the gym like the students from Dr. Nagai's school," suggested Isaac.

"I agree, but let's start right here in Hiroshima," Mai argued. "Let's see what we learn when we visit the Hiroshima junior high school student leaders' meeting next week. Hiroshima schools must have peace programs, too."

"Right," Serene said. "They must have traditions, too. Also we'll find out if Hiroshima and Nagasaki students get together."

"But where are the monuments at schools in Hiroshima?" Kino asked.

"At Sadako's school," said Isaac. "And the children's monument and student worker monument in Peace Park."

"Yes," said Kino, "but we know every school within a mile radius of Peace Park, and I don't know of any monuments at schools. Dean? Isaac?"

"You're right," Dean said.

"We'll find out. And the same with ceremonies and peace curriculums," Isaac said.

"So much to do," Andrea said. "I wish I could stay another year."

"Me too," Raina said. "I guess we'll just have to work for peace in every way we can in every place we are the rest of our lives."

"We will," Mai said.

"Yes, we are. Right now!" Raina said. "But I can't get over the fact that I'm moving to the Middle East in a few months and there people are killing each other over politics and religion, people whose religions share similar prophets and holy places."

"My grandparents say real peace will come to the world

only when all religions learn to respect and appreciate each other," said Isaac. "Then there might be authentic peace, but we still have to work at it, person to person, every day."

"Like Nagai sensei did, day by day, hour by hour, minute by minute," Andrea reminded them.

"It's an attitude, a way of living," said Raina.

"It's the metaphor we must live by," Mai suggested. "This is our way."

"Oasis of Peace," Alina and Emma sang out together.

❧ Presenting the Idea

Class members showed up at the World Friendship Center at 6:30 for the Friday evening Friendship Night. They were greeted by Dr. Harada, Hiroshima's peace activist plastic surgeon, well known for his work with both the Hiroshima Maidens and Vietnamese children who had been maimed and disfigured by napalm. Bob and Mary, directors of the Center, were there on leave from their Church of the Brethren in Canada. Each year a couple from the Peace churches—Brethren, Quaker, or Mennonite—staff the Center, which provides food and lodging for hundreds of peace activists from around the world. The Center also sponsors English language classes and peacemaking fellowships.

The Center was founded in the 1960s by peace activist Barbara Reynolds, Methodist missionary Mary McMillan, Dr. Harada, and several of the Hiroshima Maidens. Dr. Enloe and Mr. Leeper were now serving on the Board of Directors. Barbara Reynolds, an anthropologist, had come to ABCC in the early sixties to work with children suffering from atomic damage physically and psychologically. She was so moved by the experience that she and her husband became peace activists and sailed their "Protest Ship" into a Pacific atomic bomb testing area, where they were arrested and caused an international incident.

By the time Friendship Night began there were forty people in the main living room areas. The group began with a prayer led by Sister Margaret, a Catholic sister from Ireland, and an incantation from Mr. Suzuki, a Buddhist priest. Then there was singing and the sharing of ideas and about the question "What is peacemaking in my personal life?" For the next half hour, people spoke when they felt like sharing a perspective or an insight.

Kawamoto-san said, "Peace only begins with oneself."

Kim spoke, "We students know peace must be the way we treat each other. But we know too that we students of the International School are called upon to go beyond ourselves."

"We're not sure," Mai added, "but we feel we should tell our home countries the story of Sadako and her classmates."

Kieko, one of the Maidens quietly said, "You must do what you are called upon to do by your peers, your God, and in your heart."

"We want to start a club, the 1000 Cranes Club, and tell kids the story of Sadako and her classmates and invite them to fold a thousand birds of peace."

"We will make a booklet and write articles for our peacemaking project," Mai said.

"And how will you pay for this?" Mr. Leeper asked.

"We will have bake sales and walkathons and sell food at the school co-op," Isaac said. "We calculate that an initial printing of 1,000 will be 60,000 yen for a forty-page black-

and-white booklet. Mailing will be 240 yen airmail per book. Flyers will be 5,000 yen for 3,500."

"Are you ready for this adventure?" Kawamoto asked. "Are you ready for all of the work and for the work of making sure it is carried on?"

"We are," Mai said. "And our school will help us keep the spirit alive."

"Then peace be with you," Keiko said, and she passed a small bamboo basket. It was full of brightly colored bits of paper, recycled candy wrappers, and gum packets. "This small paper crane is a symbol of friendship and peacemaking. May God be with you."

And so with the blessing of those at the Friendship Night and their own sense of purpose, the students began the 1000 Cranes Club that fall evening. Together they folded cranes for the next hour as stories of faith and the work of peacemaking were told by those gathered on that lovely evening.

☙ The Club Takes Shape

Raina and Kim asked that the class begin its final planning meeting for the Club first with a note from Dean's mom and dad and then with the reading of a letter from Ms. Shibama that was included in Raina's report. Dean read,

> Dear class members. I want to congratulate you on your work and the strong research and studies you have accomplished. And now your Club. What a wonderful idea to tell Sadako's story to other children and to invite them to recycle papers and send a thousand birds of peace to where ever they may be needed. You have moti-

vated us and our friend Koyoko Yoshida to translate Mr. Masamoto Nasu's book published last year, *Orizuru no kodomotachi into* English. Our title is *Children of the Paper Crane: The Story of Sadako Sasaki and Her Struggle with the A-bomb Disease*.

In your research did you discover that on June 21, 1958, several months after the unveiling of the children's statue, a film came out titled *A Thousand Cranes*? It was produced by Kyodo Film Company and was filmed entirely in Hiroshima. Seventy Hiroshima junior high students appeared in it, including many of Sadako's friends as well as professional actors from the Tokyo Children's Theater. It's about an hour long and tells the story of Sadako and her death, how the students created leaflets they presented to the school principals' conference, and the activities of the students' Association for Peace. The last shot of the film is the statue for children of the A-bomb. I'm working to secure a copy of the film and then I will ask Mr. Kawamoto to join us to watch it and talk about your future Club.

Best wishes in peace,
Steve and Elizabeth

"That will be great," said Mai.

"I remember Mr. Kawamoto mentioning the film," commented Dean.

"Was there also a TV series?" asked Junior.

"I don't think so," replied Isaac.

"I can't keep all the groups straight from Sadako's friends and their Paper Crane Club and the Association for Peace and others," complained Kino.

"Lots of people got involved at different times in different ways," explained Dean.

RAINA HAD INTERVIEWED Ms. Shibama at her home. Emily, Kim, Isaac, Dean, and Niraj had gone with her. Kim spoke about the visit: "She was eighty years old and so genki[6] we couldn't believe her spunk. She wore a dark kimono and her hair was in a bun. She had retired from Jogakuin[7] years ago, but she was still active in the peace movement. She and Miss Macmillan, Mr. Kawamoto's mentor, were good friends. We told her about our ideas for the Club and peacemaking, and so she said she'd give us her ideas to support our project." Then Kim turned to Raina.

"Here is my report," said Raina as she passed out pages to everybody, then sat back as they took a few minutes to read "Shibama sensei—Peacemaker Teacher."

Her name is Tazu Shibama. She told us about her name. In Japanese 'ta' is rice paddy and 'zu' is the crane. In Japanese, she said, the crane has a special meaning. It is a symbol of peace and love. She was the youngest of four sisters. When she was born she was very small and not healthy. But her father wanted her to be a happy child. So he named her 'ta-zu' or 'crane in the field' because he wanted her to have a happy childhood and be peaceful and loved by everybody.

"Many people ask me why my English is so good," she said. "So I will tell you. I was a high school English teacher at Hiroshima Jogakuin. That means Hiroshima Girls School. I first learned English when I was twelve years old. My father sent me to the missionary school not far from here. It was run by the Methodist Church. I have been speaking English a very long time." She was over eighty years old now.

---

6. *Genki* means lively.
7. A Methodist girls' high school.

When she finished high school at Jogakuin, which was a Methodist school, she went to America in 1930, first to Wesleyan College, a Methodist College in Macon, Georgia. She said, "When I was a little older my teacher told me I should learn English better to become a better teacher. She said I should go again to America. But my father was a poor schoolteacher and he had little money for me to travel. So the Methodist Church arranged for my travel monies. That's how I ended up at George Peabody Teachers College in Nashville, Tennessee because Nashville was headquarters for the Methodist Church. So I can speak to you in English, in your own words, to you in your language."

She asked us to speak with her in Japanese and we did. She served green tea and cookies with bean paste. Then she said, "Well, now I would like to tell you what happened on August 6 when the bomb fell. It was eight o'clock and I was eating breakfast. I was all alone in the house. I had sent my father and sister to the country, because he was already old and the city is a hard place for old people to be during wartime. I wanted to join them, but my neighbors told me, 'Tazu, it's okay if your house burns down if a bomb fell. But our houses are so close together they will catch fire too. You must stay in your house so you can put out the fire right away if it catches fire.'

"So I was alone in my house. I was eating my breakfast. It was usual on Sunday for me to be at school at 8:00, but we were usually excused to go to school an hour late if the air raid sirens went off in the night. That night, the sirens had gone off three times. Each time we had to put on heavy clothing and run to the bomb shelter. So we ran back and forth three times that night. I was exhausted. We were excused an hour so we could get some rest. Each time we ran to the shelter we wore heavy clothes. But it was too hot in August to keep them on, so when I was eating breakfast all I had was a very simple dress and a towel on my lap. She paused and looked out the window and then began slowly to speak.

"Suddenly I saw a bright flash, but I heard nothing. In Japanese we call the bomb 'pikka-don.' 'Pikka' means bright flash and 'don' is the great sound it makes afterward. My father in the country some ten miles away heard the big sound. But we heard nothing. Afterward they told us that the big sound was too big for our ears to catch. Suddenly, I was crushed beneath my house. I thought, 'Oh God, I think I'm going to die here. All alone, crushed underneath my house.'

"But then I heard somebody moving close to me. I was very surprised because I thought I was alone underneath my house. It was my next-door neighbor, Mr. Marehara. He was standing in his garden fifty meters from me, but the blast of the bomb blew him instantly next to me. Together we were able to get out from under the house. That is why we were not burned. I was able to get out before the house started to burn. But his house was already on fire. He went running to his house, but it was too much heat and fire. He could not save his children and wife. They were all burned. They all died, all of them, dead."

Then she stopped. "Can you listen to more?" she asked us. We nodded. She continued.

"When I got out of the house I looked all around. I was shocked. I could see the mountains. Where there had been buildings that blocked the mountains, now everything was flattened and burning and there was all the smoke and dust. But above it you could see blue sky and the mountains. Now I could see all around, for everything was flat. I began walking, not knowing what was happening. I was going to get way from this, I thought.

I went to the train station. There were no trains. Everything was burning. And everywhere people were burned and dead. So I started walking. All around me there were other people walking too. But they were all quiet. The whole city was quiet, not a sound. The people were like ghosts walking. I think the shock was too great. We could not say a word."

She paused and took a deep, quiet breath.

"Many of them had their hands hanging down, with the skin falling off. Many of them had no clothes, for they burned instantly and fell off. Many boys had only a belt on or boots. Nothing left. Many mothers had babies on their backs, but babies were dead. But the mothers did not know it. The shock was too great."

She was again quiet. I asked, "Did you make it home?"

"Yes," she nodded. "It took me over a year to get better because I had some poisoning from the bomb. But I became healthy. But the people who stayed in the city, they were not so lucky. They had to breathe poison air and drink poisoned water and eat poisoned food. The food was so scarce. They had no choice but to eat and drink and breathe the radiation poisoned food and water or die anyway. So they did. Pretty soon, their gums began to bleed and their hair fell out. They never stopped bleeding. You see most, stayed in the city to try to find their families: their children, their husbands and wives, their parents, their friends, their lovers. They did not know what kind of bomb it was. They did not understand about the nuclear poison.

"I went to my school the next day. It was totally destroyed. At our school we had 700 girl students. Because it was wartime, the 16- to 18-year-olds had to work in the factories making weapons. So I had the younger children, ages 13 to 15. All of them who stayed at the school died instantly. When the bomb fell I lost all of them, good friends, 18 teachers and 350 students. All died, all were killed instantly. And for days afterward other students died every day, some in my arms."

She stopped, looked out the window toward the mountains, and then turned to us. "You must do your work. It is your responsibility. You came to live here and to discover the secrets of Hiroshima.

Now you must be peacemakers and stewards of the earth and all the people. So start your club and let it spread all over."

She stopped and handed us a sheet of paper. "I want you to have this. It is what I tell people when I travel the world speaking for world peace and the abolition of nuclear weapons. It is a message from my girls to the world: No More Hiroshimas. Let the dove reign."

Then she said to us, "I am sure that the ones who died have much to say. But they have no mouths to speak. As I can speak, and speak a little English, I think it is my duty to bring you this message: War is no good. War does not solve anything. Bombs, no matter how big they are, cannot give the answer. The only thing that can bring the answer is peace and happiness and friendship."

"Then she said good-bye and hugged us," Raina said.

"It was powerful. I'll never forget it," added Dean.

"Me either," Emily concluded.

14

Birds of Peace

Raina began to speak. "I came here several months ago, and in a few months I will be moving on to Israel. I've learned so much and I'm not even sure what all I've learned. So I've tried to write down some of my thoughts in a poem." She cleared her throat, looked upward and then down at her paper as she began to read:

Birds of Peace

This island sits like a diamond in the sun.
From there is seen the whole world,
calling God's name to draw her near.
Birds of peace circling from above,
crying from the eagle, cooing from the dove,
and then it lands and settles down at our school—
an Oasis of Peace—
that same oasis I find in my heart wherever I am.
Peace does begin with me,
and others have found it in the now silence of Auschwitz
and Anne Frank's home,
in the internment and concentrations camps of American
citizens in my hometown,

at the Cenotaph among all the doves of Peace Park,
and then by the river I found it was within and between ourselves—
an Oasis of Peace.
When doves were crying
Martin Luther King told us the simple truth:
"The world is more and more a neighborhood.
But is it any more of a humanhood?
If we don't learn to live together as brothers and sisters we will perish together as fools."
These small paper birds of peace, folded with our hands
for the world to know
that children want peace—
they teach us that learning to fold a paper bird,
a crane or dove,
is like becoming a peacemaker.
You make mistakes.
You start over.
You learn from others.
You don't do it alone.
So with our Oasis of Peace,
built and nurtured out of evil and the ashes.
And so the doves cried.
Oasis of Peace

"Beautiful," Mai whispered.

"I think it says what we're all feeling," Isaac added.

"I like the Martin Luther King part too," Johann said.

"And the idea about paper folding and peacemaking," Mr. Morris asked, "Where did that come from?"

Raina replied, "Serene, in Mrs. Enloe's class, told me that

last week. She's seven and when she went to Japanese school she learned all kinds of paper folding. She said she taught her mom and dad the crane."

"The Oasis of Peace is such a cool idea," Kim said.

"Peace of mind," Dean added.

"Internal peace," said Mai. "Prince's music, too—'When Doves Cry.'"

"Well," Raina explained, "I got the idea from the place I'm moving to next in Israel. It's called the Oasis of Peace."

"Does it have date trees and water?" asked Johann.

"No," replied Raina. "It's not in that kind of desert, and its sits on a hill."

"Why the name then?" asked Isaac.

"Because the village is called Neve Shalom and Wahat Al-Salam in Hebrew and Arabic. It is a cooperative village of Israeli Arabs and Jews who own the village together. So far it is the only village like this. They create a community based on tolerance and respect by working together. And yet each family remains Muslim or Jewish in their culture and religion." Raina had read much about this special place.

"That's great idea," said Junior, "this Oasis of Peace."

"They've been nominated many times for the Nobel Peace Prize," said Raina.

"Maybe our club will too," Nicole commented.

"Well, they have worked many years, very hard. They sponsor a School of Peace that has brought more than fifteen thousand Jewish and Palestinian teenagers together to share. They first must get ready at their schools and then they come together for four days to develop a dialogue and understand each other." Raina had never visited, but her dad had been there several times and had told her about it.

"They become peacemakers?" Isaac asked.

"They begin the process. They usually come with many stereotypes and actually hating not trusting each other," Raina said.

"Isn't it amazing," Isaac pondered. "Christians, Jews, and Muslims worshipping the same God in the same place and yet hating each other."

"History," Mia added. "People's inhumanity to people. It's all of history."

"Human imperfection," Dean said. "War is evil."

"It's crazy," Mai said. "But is war sometimes a necessary evil?"

"The whole world is crazy," Emily declared. "M.A.D. means not only uncivilized nuclear war but local wars too. Like Israel and Palestine."

"After meeting four times," Raina continued her story, "the students often at least tolerate each other. Some still hate. Some are suspicious. But some respect each other and become friends."

"Everywhere we are we must all make an oasis of peace inside ourselves and with the people in our particular place," Mai said.

"Shalom," Raina said quietly. "Shalom is Peace."

"Shalom," everyone repeated.

"Shalom," Raina whispered. "Pray for peace, that it becomes necessary, and not war and hatred."

"Heiwa," said Dean.

"Heiwa." Everyone repeated the Japanese word for peace. And then there was silence and the room was full of words and feelings in the head and heart.

❧ This Place Called Hiroshima

"I need to read my poem," Kim said. "This is for all of us and a special message for Raina. And I love the Prince of Peace's music too. 'When Doves Cry'? Wow!" From her pocket she pulled a neatly folded paper, unfolded it, cleared her voice, waited a moment, and read:

In this place called Hiroshima,
there is an island where all kids feel safe
and inspired to help our world.
It is a place where you will sit down next to her,
next to the human being who is laughed at
and called names just because she talks different, looks different,
walks different, thinks different
acts different.
You will sit down next to her and befriend her,
because when you get to know each other,
you find out you are pretty much the same
about a lot of things.
You feel and you laugh
and you cry like the cranes and doves.
You have dreams and you have hopes,
for you want to be a friend
and you want to have a friend.
For all of you
know what it is like to be treated differently
because you are labeled a color
or a gender or a nation or a culture

while riding the same little blue marble of a planet
spinning and spinning, around and around
in search of places that are oases,
places where doves coo in the hands of children.
Shalom. Heiwa. Oasis of Peace

❧ A Thousand Paper Cranes

The students were as good as their word; they published their booklet about Sadako soon after Friendship Night. The booklet also described the children's club that was established after Sadako's death to work for peace. It was published on October 25, 1985, thirty years to the day of Sadako's death. The idea of folding paper birds, cranes or doves, has taken many forms in the helping hands and hearts of people around the world. The following article, from the original booklet produced by the International School students, also appeared by invitation from the United Nations in the *UNESCO Courier* in August 1986, the International Year of Peace.

1000 Cranes Club

Spread your wings, and we'll fly away.
—Sadako Sasaki

This story starts in 1945. A girl named Sadako Sasaki was living in a Japanese city called Hiroshima, along with about half a million other people. When she was two years old, the first atomic bomb ever to be used against human beings was dropped on Hiroshima. Most of the city was completely smashed and burned to the ground. Sadako was about a mile and a half away from where the bomb exploded, but she wasn't burned or injured at all, at least not in any way people could see.

A few weeks after the bomb, people in Hiroshima began dying from a sickness even the doctors couldn't understand. People who seemed perfectly healthy would suddenly get weak and sick and then just die. It was so strange and new that no one knew what to do to a particular person.

By the time Sadako was in the seventh grade, she was a normal, happy twelve-year-old girl going to a regular school and studying and playing like everyone else. Ten years had passed since the bomb and she was thinking about other things. One of the things she thought about most was running.

One day after an important relay race that she helped her team win, she felt tired and dizzy. After a while she felt better, so she thought it was just that she was so tired because of the race. Over the next few weeks she tried to forget about it, but the dizziness kept coming back, especially when she was running. She didn't tell anyone about it, not even Chizuko, her best friend. Finally, one morning, it got so bad that she fell down and just lay on the ground for a while. This time everyone noticed. They took her to the Red Cross hospital to see what was the matter. No one could believe what they found out. Sadako had leukemia, a kind of cancer of the blood. At that time quite a few children about Sadako's age were getting leukemia, which the people then called "the A-bomb disease." Almost everyone who got the disease died, and Sadako was very scared. She didn't want to die.

Soon after Sadako went to the hospital, Chizuko came to visit her. She brought some special paper and folded a paper crane. Chizuko told Sadako about a legend. She said that the crane, a sacred bird in Japan, lives for a thousand years, and if a sick person folds a thousand cranes, that person will get well. Sadako decided to fold a thousand cranes. Because of the leukemia she often felt too weak and tired, so she couldn't work all the time, but from that day on, whenever she could, she folded cranes.

Sadako actually folded her thousand cranes, but she wasn't getting any better. But instead of getting angry or giving up, she decided she would fold more cranes. She started on her second thousand. Everyone was amazed by how brave and patient she was. On October 25, 1955, surrounded by her loving family, she went to sleep, peacefully, for the last time.

But this story doesn't end with Sadako's death. She had a lot of friends who loved her and who missed her very much. And they didn't only feel sad about Sadako. Lots of other children in Hiroshima had died or were dying of the A-bomb disease. Her friends wanted very much to do something for Sadako. So thirty-nine of her classmates formed a club and began asking for money for a monument for her. The word spread quickly. Students from 3,100 schools in Japan and from nine other countries gave money, and finally, on May 5, 1958, almost three years after Sadako died, they got enough money to build the monument. It's called the Children's Peace Monument and it is in the Peace Park, which is in the middle of Hiroshima, right where the atomic bomb was dropped.

The movement to build this monument became so famous and popular that a movie called *A Thousand Paper Cranes* was made about it. About sixty children from Hiroshima and about twenty children from Tokyo helped make the movie, and when it was finished they wanted to stay together as friends, so they started a new club called "The Paper Crane Club." The purpose of this club was to help children get together to think and work for peace. This club has continued to exist for almost thirty years. The members take care of Sadako's monument and visit atomic bomb survivors, people who were in Hiroshima when the bomb was dropped, and people who are getting sick and old or who just need help for some reason.

One other thing they always do is fold cranes. They use the

cranes in many ways. Sometimes they hang them on Sadako's monument and other monuments in Hiroshima's Peace Park. Sometimes they send them to world leaders as a way of reminding those leaders that the children of the world want to get rid of nuclear bombs. And whenever world leaders or atomic bomb survivors or people working for peace come to Hiroshima, members of the Paper Crane Club greet them and put a wreath of cranes around their necks to welcome them and to help them think about the meaning of Hiroshima.

But the meaning of folding cranes and the meaning of Hiroshima and the Paper Crane Club are perhaps best summed up in the words carved on the granite base of the Children's Peace Monument:

> THIS IS OUR CRY
> THIS IS OUR PRAYER
> TO BUILD PEACE IN THIS WORLD

15

The 1000 Cranes Club

Extensions and Interconnections

The students discovered more and more materials. They found Robert Jungk's 1959 book in German *Strahlen aus der Asche* (Children of the Ashes), which is a biography of the rebirth of Hiroshima and includes a section on Mr. Kawamoto, Sadako, and the formation of the Thousand Cranes Movement and later the Youth Movement for Peace. Dean and Yoshio's parents, Elizabeth Baldwin and Steve Leeper, with friend Kyoko Yoshida, kept their promise to the students and completed their translation of Masamoto Nasu's *Orizuru no kodomotachi* (1984) as *Children of the Paper Cranes: The Story of Sadako Sasaki and Her Struggle with the A-Bomb Disease.*

Since 1985, thousands of booklets have been sent to schools and organizations in more than thirty countries. Students in hundreds of schools and classrooms have sent a thousand cranes to be placed at monuments in Peace Park.

There have been many wonderful spin-offs of this project, which have fostered creativity in children and their teachers and promoted relationships among many groups of people. Besides sending colorful banners to accompany their cranes, groups have sent to Hiroshima hundreds of drawings, dioramas, collages, an original play, several video letters, tapes of songs (including original works), poetry, and stories —all expressions of the human spirit to create, to reach out, and to touch others. Numerous classrooms and schools and groups have linked with each other—in some cases classrooms within a building; in others, across town, a region, or a nation, and between nations.

In Argentina, schools throughout the country sent cranes and then began exchanging students and projects with each other. In West Germany a participating school created a cultural information exchange (videos, artwork) with a 1000 Cranes Club school in Sweden. In Sweden a children's agency published articles on the club in more than fifty magazines and newspapers. In St. Paul, Minnesota, a class of second graders, with help from Ken Simon, introduced Sadako's story to classes of eleventh graders and taught them to fold cranes. In Argentina, Brazil, Mexico, and India, groups translated parts of the 1000 Cranes Club booklet into native languages and shared the story with other students. In Townsville, Australia, the whole town, led by the mayor, joined to have a picnic and fold paper cranes to send to Hiroshima.

Inspired by Sadako's story, third graders at Arroyo del Oso Elementary School in Albuquerque, New Mexico, decided to raise money to erect a "sister" children's peace statue in Los Alamos, New Mexico, the test site for the bomb. Children and teenagers in New Mexico formed the Kids' Committee to oversee the project and raised enough money to complete the monument.

In 1986 the 1000 Cranes Project became part of the International School's activities (which involved endless correspondence and delivery of cranes to Peace Park). Then over the next two years students exchanged culture boxes and arts and crafts with students in a small school in Pigeon Forge, Tennessee, as well as video letters with other international schools in Japan, including travelogues and videos on indigenous folk dances and songs. Students exchanged a how-to video with a school in Australia (the Australians sent a tape on Aussie rules of football and the correct way to throw a boomerang and enclosed three boomerangs).

From a school in East Germany students received fifty drawings of children and scenes of peace, each under half a rainbow. International School students completed the rainbows, drew scenes under the other half, photocopied the drawings, and sent the originals back to East Germany, where the two halves were displayed.

Over the years the Hiroshima International School students have raised the funds to translate the Sadako story into Japanese, Spanish, and Russian. In 1987 Gorbachev sent students a telegram of encouragement. Many teachers have written to Hiroshima International School, describing how this project encourages children (and adults) to enact social values not often given preference in our competitive, individualistic educational system by encouraging students to work together in a communal atmosphere of cooperation for a common good and for the joy inherent in the task of creating. Children tacitly show adults how much they care to work together.

In the original 1000 Cranes Club booklet written by the children (who are now adults), Kim wrote:

Something we have learned from folding 1000 cranes is that even with a group of twenty-five students, it takes time to fold a 1000. In a class of twenty-five, each student would first have to learn to fold a crane and then fold forty. But once you begin, it can be fun. Most important, it is a time to work together, to talk about things like friendship and conflicts. We don't have any particular suggestions other than when we did this, we learned a lot about each other, we helped each other, and now our class is really close. We folded these cranes for peace and in memory of Sadako, but really we helped ourselves. Please join us.

For information about joining the 1000 Cranes Club project, send a self-addressed, stamped envelope to Walter Enloe, Graduate School, Hamline University, 1536 Hewitt Ave., St. Paul, MN 55104, or check the Hiroshima International School's Web site on the Internet.

❧ Reflections from Dr. Enloe

I hold two recurring images inspired by this project as it has evolved over the years. One is that everything is interconnected and systemic. I look at a photograph of the Earth taken from outer space, and I see a new paradigm for what it means to be human. I'll tell you its secret. It's not the information-processing system the scientistic education establishment wants us to believe in—new machinery in an outdated model. No, our photograph is of a cultural *umwelt* or an ecosystem, but not simply images of a food web or a water-oxygen cycle. Our paradigm includes two children, a boy and girl, one from the United States and one from Japan, sitting on the beach on a sunny day, alive and connected, and folding cranes.

The second image is one of being human. It speaks for all of us committed to children as active creators, experimenters, and citizens, locally and globally. I share with my mentor Jean Piaget the deep respect he had for children and hold to his conviction that

> the principal goal of education is to create people who are capable of doing new things, not simply repeating what other generations have done—people who are creators, inventors, and discoverers. The second goal of education is to form minds that are critical, can verify, and do not accept everything they are offered. The great danger today is from slogans, collective opinions, ready-made trends of thought. We have to be able to resist individually, to criticize, to distinguish between what is proven and what is not. So we need pupils who are active, who learn early to find out for themselves, partly by their own spontaneous activity and partly through the materials we set up for them; who learn early to tell what is verifiable and what is simply the first idea to come to them.

I ask you to join me in Nagasaki and Hiroshima's Peace Park—today or in a hundred years. Imagine! We stand facing the Children's Monument, dedicated to all of those thousands of children, who, like Sadako, died from the effects of the A-bomb and the millions and millions of fellow human beings who have died in war and civil strife. We step forward to the monument and place our cranes at its base and read the inscription:

> THIS IS OUR CRY
> THIS IS OUR PRAYER
> TO BUILD PEACE IN THIS WORLD

Resources

Books for Older Students and Adults

A-Bomb: A City Tells Its Story, edited by Yoshiteru Kosake, translated by Kiyoko Kageyama, Kaoru Ogura, and Charlotte Susu-Maho. Hiroshima Peace and Culture Foundation, Hiroshima.

A Place Called Hiroshima, by Betty Jean Lifton, published by Kodansha International, New York.

Atomic Aftermath, edited by Kenzaburo Oe, published by Shueisha.

The Atomic Bomb: Voices from Hiroshima and Nagasaki, edited by Kyoko Seldon, published by M. E. Sharpe, 1997.

At Work in the Fields of the Bomb, by Robert Del Tredici, published by Harper & Row, New York.

The Bells of Nagasaki, by Takashi Nagai, published by Kodansha, Tokyo, and Kodansha International, New York, 1984.

Black Rain, by Masuji Ibuse, translated by John Baxter, published by Kodansha International, New York.

Children of the Ashes, by Robert Jungk, published by Harcourt Brace & World, New York, 1959.

Children of the Paper Crane, by Masamoto Nasu, published by M. E. Sharpe, New York, 1991.

City of Silence: Listening to Hiroshima, by Rachelle Linner, published by Orbis Books, 1995.

The Day Man Lost, by the Pacific War Research Society, published by Kodansha International, New York.

Death in Life: The Survivors of Hiroshima, by Robert Lifton, published by Simon & Schuster, New York.

Fire from the Ashes: Short Stories about Hiroshima and Nagasaki, edited by Kenzaburo Oe, published by Readers International, 1985.

Hibakusha: Survivors of Hiroshima and Nagasaki, published by Kosei, Tokyo.

Hiroshima, by John Hersey, published by Bantam, New York.

Hiroshima: Three Witnesses, by Richard Minear and Toge Sankichi, published by Princeton University Press, 1995.

Hiroshima: Why America Dropped the Bomb, by Ronald Takaki, published by BackBay Books, San Francisco, 1996.

Hiroshima and Nagasaki and *The Impact of the A-bomb, Hiroshima and Nagasaki, 1945–1985* (abridged version), compiled by the Committee for the Compilation of Materials on Damage Caused by the Atomic Bombs in Hiroshima and Nagasaki, translated by Eisei Ishikawa and David L. Swain, published by Iwanami Shoten.

Hiroshima and Nagasaki: Retrospect and Prospect, edited by D. Holdstock and F. Barnaby, published by Frank Cass, New York, 1995.

Hiroshima and Nagasaki through the Eyes of the American Journalists, by the Hiroshima International Cultural Foundation, published by the Akiba Project, 1984.

Hiroshima Diary (the journal of a Japanese physician, Aug. 6 to Sept. 30, 1945), by Michiko Hachiya, translated by Warner Wells, published by University of North Carolina Press, Chapel Hill.

Hiroshima Handbook, by the Hiroshima Interpreters for Peace, Hiroshima.

Hiroshima in America: Fifty Years of Denial, by Robert Jay Lifton, published by Avon Press, 1996.

Hiroshima in History and Memory, edited by Michael Hogan, published by Cambridge University Press, 1996.

Hiroshima in Memoriam and Today, by Hitoshi Takayama.

Hiroshima Notes, by Kenzaburo Oe, published by YMCA Press, Tokyo.

Hiroshima Peace Reader, by Yoshiteru Kosaki, translated by Alice Ruth Ramseyer, Robert Ramseyer, Akira Tashiro, and Nichiko Tashiro, published by Hiroshima Peace Culture Foundation, Hiroshima.

Hiroshima's Shadow, edited by Kai Bird, published by Pamphleteers Press, 1998.

The Hiroshima Story, by Toshi Maruki, published by A & C Black.

Hiroshima Surgeon, by Tomin Harada, translated by Alice R. Ramseyer and Robert Ramseyer, published by Faith and Life Press.

The Making of the Atomic Bomb, by Richard Rhodes, published by Simon & Schuster, New York.

The Mushroom Cloud, by Fumiko Kaya, translated by Ryoji Kumagawa.

The Nuclear Holocaust, by Kazuo Chugo, translated by Asaki Shinbu.

The Pathology of Power, by Norman Cousins, published by Norton, New York.

On the Wings of Peace: In Memory of Hiroshima and Nagasaki, edited by Sheila Hamanaka, published by Clarion Books, New York, 1995.

The Other Hiroshima: Korean A-Bomb Victims Tell Their Story, by Paksu Nam, translated by Greg Barrett, Bill Healy, Warren Hesse, and Phil Hill.

Peace Declarations, by the Mayors of Hiroshima, published by the Hiroshima Peace Culture Foundation, Hiroshima.

"Peaceful Paper Cranes," by Walter Enloe in *Learning by Giving: K–8 Service Learning*, edited by Rich Cairns, published by National Youth Leaderhsip Council, St. Paul, Minn.

The Road from Hiroshima by Marc Kaminski, published by Simon & Schuster, New York.

Ruin from the Air: The Atomic Mission to Hiroshima, by Gordon Thomas, published by Hamish Hamilton, London, 1977.

"Sadako and the Thousand Cranes Club," by Walter Enloe in *An Instructional Guide to Teaching about the United Nations*, edited by James Muldoon and Mary Eileen Sorenson, published by UNA-USA, New York.

The Songs of Hiroshima (an anthology of songs and poems in Japanese and English), edited and translated by Miyao Ohara, published by Satsuki Shuppan.

Strahlen aus der Asche (Children of the Ashes: The Story of a Rebirth), by Robert Jungk, published by Alfred Verlag, Berlin.

"The Thousand Cranes Club," by Walter Enloe in ***Linking through Diversity,*** edited by Walter Enloe and Ken Simon, published by Zephyr Press, Tucson.

Testimonies of Hiroshima and Nagasaki, edited by Suguru Matsuki, translated by Earl Bergh, published by the Committee for Peace and Nuclear Disarmament.

White Town Hiroshima, by Yasuko Kimura, translated by Nobuko Ueno and Jerri Okada, published by Bunka Hyoron.

❧ Children's Books

The Angry Jizo, by Yuko Yamaguchi, translated by Beth Harrison and Hisashi Oda, published by Yamaguchi Shoten.

Birds of Peace, by Walter Enloe and others, published by United Nations Association, St. Paul, Minn., and Afton Press.

Birds of Peace: Building Community and a Peaceful World, by Walter Enloe, published by Whitewing Press, San Francisco.

Children of Hiroshima (accounts by students), edited by Arata Osada, published by Harper & Row, New York.

Hiroshima, by Laurence Yap, published by Apple, New York, 1995.

Hiroshima: The Shadow of the Bomb, by Richard Tames, published by Heineman Library, 2001.

Hiroshima and Nagasaki, by S. Ishikawa, published by Basic Books, New York, 1992.

Hiroshima and Nagasaki, Cornerstones of Freedom, by Barbara Feinberg, published by Childrens Press, New York, 1995.

Hiroshima and Nagasaki: New Perspectives, by R. G. Grant, published by Steck/Vaughn, 1998.

Hiroshima No Pika, by Nancy H. Tunison, published by Kagyusha.

In the Sky over Nagasaki: A Peace Reader for Children, published by the Nagasaki Prefecture Hibakusha Teachers Association (translated 1983; Wilmington College Peace Resource Center).

I Saw It, I Saw It, by Keiji Nakazawa, published by Educomics.

Little Mary, the Blue-Eyed Doll, by Eiko Takeda, translated by Michael Toyama and J. Littlemore, published by Yamaguchi Shoten.

Living Beneath the Atomic Cloud: Testimony of the Children of Nagasaki, compiled by Dr. Takashi Nagai, 1945 (translated 1984; Wilmington College Peace Resource Center).

My Mother Died in Hiroshima, by Yuko Matsumoto, translated by Akira Matsuo, published by the Hiroshima Peace Culture Foundation, Hiroshima.

Peace Crane, by Sheila Hamanaka, published by Morrow Junior Books, 1995.

Sadako, by Eleanor Coerr, published by G. P. Putnam, New York, 1993.

Sadako and the Thousand Paper Cranes, by Eleanor Coerr, published by G. P. Putnam & Sons and by Yamaguchi Shoten.

The Thousand Cranes Club, by Walter Enloe and Steve Leeper, published by Hiroshima Center for Conflict Resolution, Hiroshima, and Afton Press.

The Twinkling Stars Know Everything, by Nagako Ikagami.

❧ Additional Resources

Barefoot Gen, Project Gen, c/o Jim Peck. War Registers League, 339 Lafayette St., New York, NY 10012.

On a Paper Crane (video)

This is an animated cartoon, created in Japan, about the abolition of nuclear arms and the importance of peace. In the story, Tomoko is a young girl living in Hiroshima. One day during her summer vacation, she visits the Hiroshima Peace Memorial alone, where she meets Sadako, who guides her on a spectacular adventure. For information on the English version write:

Peace Anime No Kai
Dokuritsu Eiga Center
7th Floor, Taiyo Building
3-16-2 Shimbashi, Minato-ku
Tokyo, Japan 100
Fax, 81-3-3432-8633

"Send Her a Thousand Cranes" by the jazz fusion band Hiroshima on their album *East* (Epic Records, 1989).

"1,000 Candles, 1,000 Cranes" by Small Potatoes (Jacquie Manning and Rich Preziosa), PO Box 315, Cary IL 60013

A Thousand Cranes (a play in one act)

Quickly becoming a children's classic, *A Thousand Cranes* tells the story of Sadako. The play, by Katherine Schultz Miller, may be ordered from:

The Dramatic Publishing Company
311 Washington St.
Woodstock, IL 60098.

Ms. Miller is Artistic Director of ArtReach Touring Theatre, whose company tours nationally, performing *A Thousand Cranes* and other plays for children and adults. For information write

ArtReach Touring Company
3074 Madison Rd.
Cincinnati, OH 45309
or call (513) 871-2300.

Peace Resource Center, Wilmington College. Barbara Reynolds founded this center at the Quaker college in 1975. For a review of their resources and programs go to their Web site or contact them at prc@wilmington.edu.

Informed Democracy offers videos, books, posters, and other material related to the Sadako story.

Storytellers Elaine Wynne and Larry Johnson can be contacted at 315 Georgia Ave., Golden Valley, MN 55427, 612-546-1074.

On the Internet

Search the Internet to find current information on the 1000 Cranes Club and Hiroshima International School's latest project to build an International Children's Monument in Hiroshima. See the Web sites for:

Hiroshima International School
Cranes for Peace
Thousand Cranes Peace Network
Sadako Peace Club
Sadako Peace Project
Informed Democracy
paperfolding.com
Nagasaki City

Nagasaki Atomic Bomb Museum (has Dr. Nagai's story)
Nagasaki Peace Declaration
Shiroyama Elementary School
Fuchi Junior High School

Also see **Sadako Peace Project**, which offers a club, music, and a curriculum.

❧ About the Author and Contributors

WALTER ENLOE is a teacher in Hamline University's Graduate School of Education. From age 12 to age 17 he lived in Japan. A graduate of Eckerd College and Emory University, he taught K–12 at the Paideia School in Atlanta and was principal and teacher at Hiroshima International School from 1980 to 1988. The aim of this book is to demonstrate a project approach to education. It is also a memoir and an autobiographical fiction of the author's lifework in Hiroshima, based on characters both real and imagined.

ISAAC ENLOE lived in Japan from age three to age eleven, worked as a counselor at Concordia College's Japanese Language Village, graduated from Carleton College and received his MAT from Lewis and Clark College. He teaches kindergarten at the Blue Oak School in Napa, California.

KATHERINE SERENE ENLOE is a student at Hamline University majoring in anthropology and minoring in religion and East Asian studies. She was a counselor at Concordia College's Japanese Language Village. Katherine Serene was born in Hiroshima; "Serene" signifies peacefulness in honor of her birthplace.

NICK KASHMAN, a junior at Avalon High School in St. Paul, contributed important research and writing on Nagasaki.

CREDITS:
Illustrations on pages 4, 52, 84, 146, and 167 by Serene Enloe.
Illustrations on pages ii, 14, 58, 77, 95, 141, 183, and 191 by Isaac Enloe.
Editing and project management by Stacey Lynn, Green Sand Press.

PRINTED IN U.S.A.